Contemporary
Whitework

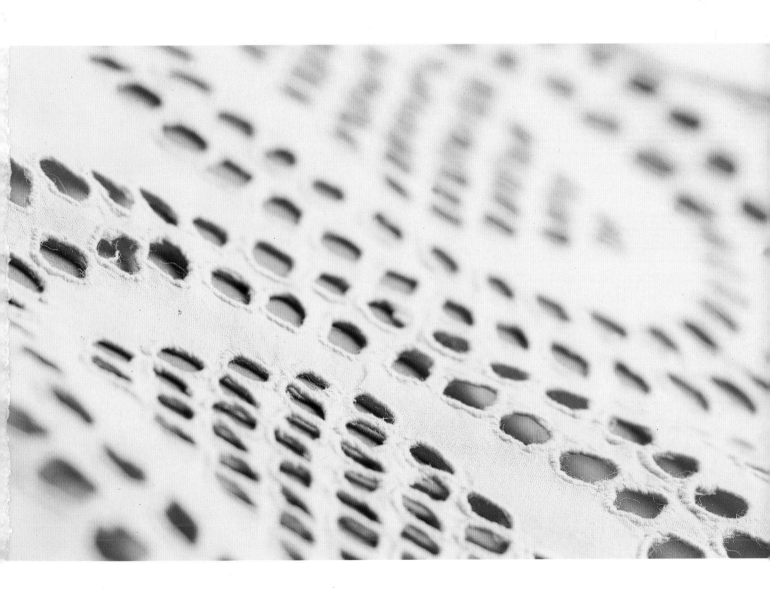

Contemporary
Whitework

Tracy A Franklin
Nicola Jarvis

Batsford

First published 2005

Text © Tracy A Franklin and Nicola Jarvis 2005

The right of Tracy A Franklin and Nicola Jarvis to be identified as
Authors of this work has been asserted by them in accordance with the
Copyright, Designs and Patents Act 1988.

Volume © B T Batsford 2005

Text on page 90 © Marée D Maher 2005

ISBN 0 7134 8964 2

A CIP catalogue record for this book is available from the British
Library.

Printed in China
for the publisher
B T Batsford
The Chrysalis Building
Bramley Road
London W10 6SP

An imprint of **Chrysalis** Books Group plc

Distributed in the United States and Canada by Sterling Publishing Co.,
387 Park Avenue South, New York, NY 10016, USA

Contents

Acknowledgements

Nikki and I would first of all like to thank Tina Persaud for approaching us to write another book for B T Batsford and Nicola Birtwisle for overseeing its progress. Our thanks also go to the Royal School of Needlework, especially to Elizabeth Elvin for loaning us part of the collection and Kirsty Simpson for organizing this. We would also like to thank the Royal School of Needlework for giving us the opportunity to learn these traditional art needlework skills and Sally Saunders for teaching us when we were apprentices.

Big thanks should be given to Celia Ankers, for the long loan of her book, and Shirley Smith, for organizing this, and to Ann Carrick, for the loan of her book. Thanks are also due to Val Stoddart, who gave me some whitework reference books, which I avidly used, and Clare Hanham, who loaned us some of her whitework samples. Massive thanks to Bridget Rylands and Marée D Maher for their proofreading and text writing, which was much needed, and to Agnes Bryson, for allowing us to use her book, *Ayrshire Needlework*, as a source of inspiration.

Nikki and I would like to give special thanks to Wendy Hogg for always being there ready to help, Pat Healy for her friendship, Vicky Hutchinson for doing all our last-minute jobs, all our contributors, without whom we could never have written this book, and Mrs Nelsson. Coats Crafts UK, DMC Creative World, Copeland Linens Limited and Mace & Nairn deserve our grateful thanks for providing us with threads, materials and catalogues. Finally, we would like to thank Anne MacKinnon for the scissors and J & J Adin for the stiletto.

Nikki would personally like to thank all her family and friends for their support, especially her mum Pat Jarvis, brother William Jarvis and nephew Jack Jarvis.

I, too, would like to thank all my family and friends for their ongoing support, with particular thanks to Margaret Elders, Alice Hirst, Enid Maughan, Anne Rand, Ros Barnes, Wendy Andrews and Vicky Hutchinson for helping me to keep my freelance business going at Fowlers Yard.

Last but not least, I would like to give my appreciation to Nikki, who has been brilliant to work with, has unbelievable talent at drawing illustrations and is so reliable and patient at all times.

Design board for shadow work (detail)
Florence Collingwood
Collection of ideas for a small design in
shadow work, using organza and paper.

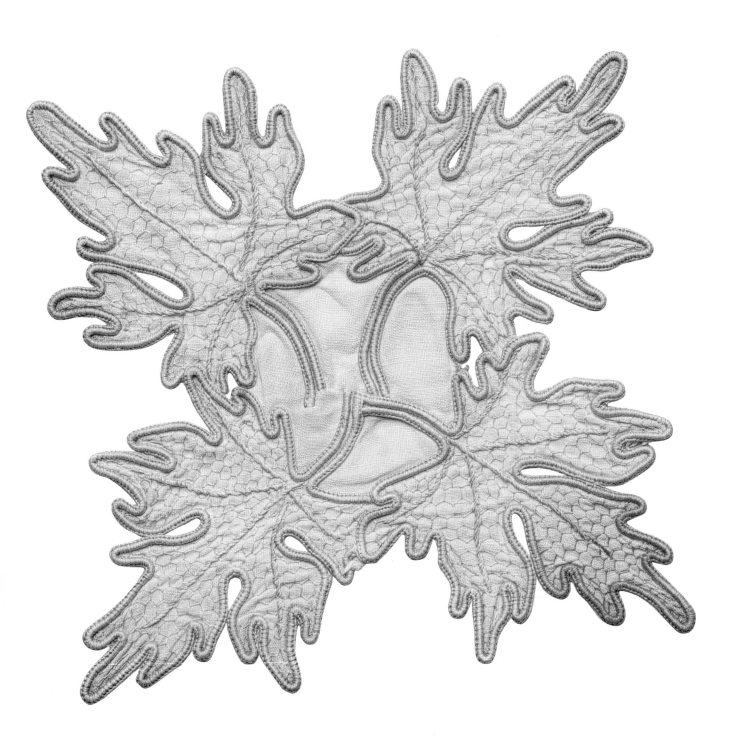

Introduction

Whitework is a general term given to many types of embroidery that were originally worked in white, using natural fabrics and materials. This book demonstrates how each basic whitework technique is worked traditionally, although using the different threads and materials available today. It shows samples and gives suggestions on how the traditional rules can be explored further to produce new and exciting effects.

Much of the whitework made throughout history decorated garments and adorned furnishings in the domestic environment. Religious establishments also commissioned whitework for ecclesiastical vestments and linens. In many Western cultures, white embroidery was used on clothing worn in key life rituals, for example on the collars, cuffs and hems of christening gowns, wedding dresses and funeral shrouds. All embroidery, including whitework, became associated with comfort, wealth and status. White embroideries, in particular, were used to embellish underclothes and nightwear.

Regional techniques and stitch patterns were passed down through the generations. These techniques were influenced by individual interpretation, economic factors and fashionable taste, as well as increasing travel to and trade with other parts of the world. In this way, characteristics from different cultures were absorbed into existing whitework styles and new techniques evolved.

Whitework embroidery styles vary considerably, from the raised stitches of Irish Mountmellick work to the lace-like intricacy of Ayrshire work from Scotland. A little investigation will soon reveal that the possibilities with whitework are endless.

While writing this book, we discovered great gaps in time where there was little information about whitework. We suspect, however, that it could not have disappeared completely, but in fact remained in existence somewhere. Possible reasons for the gaps may be that records were lost or destroyed; printing processes may not have been developed, or people were illiterate and techniques were passed on by word of mouth, in a similar way to stories and legends. This led us to conclude that, like many embroidery techniques, whitework is the 'people's embroidery', coming as it does from all walks of life. For this reason, we would like to dedicate this book to all those who have contributed, past and present.

For this book, we invited embroiderers and textile artists to go beyond the limitations of traditional whitework. Their individual approaches to the different traditions are fascinating, combining unlikely threads and fabrics with innovative designs to produce inspiring interpretations of the basic techniques, some more traditional than others.

When trying out some of these ideas, basic stitch patterns can be used as a starting point. Coloured and novelty threads or fabrics can be used instead of white ones, and unusual designs can be explored to see how traditional techniques may be adapted. The most important thing is to have fun experimenting with these beautiful techniques. They are the legacy of at least two thousand years of whitework.

Tablemat

Small tablemat worked on linen fabric using cutwork and surface embroidery.

Tools and equipment

Needles

It is important to have the correct needle when stitching whitework embroidery, the correct choice depending on the whitework technique to be used.

Broderie anglaise and **Richelieu/cutwork** both require fine crewel needles, with long eyes and fine points; 8–10 are the best sizes, depending on the scale and thread size used.

Drawn thread work requires two needle types. The first is a tapestry needle, required for withdrawing the threads and reworking in the decoration. This is used because it has a blunt point, which helps guide the thread through the holes of the fabric rather than piercing it. Use sizes 20–24, depending on the gauge of the evenweave fabric and the thread size. A crewel embroidery needle is used for the buttonholing at the ends of the borders to secure the threads that have been withdrawn and woven back. Sizes 8 or 9 are used, depending on the thread size.

Pulled work is worked on an evenweave fabric and requires a needle that will pull the threads through the holes of the fabric without piercing them. A tapestry needle, size 20–24, is therefore used, depending on the scale of the fabric and thread.

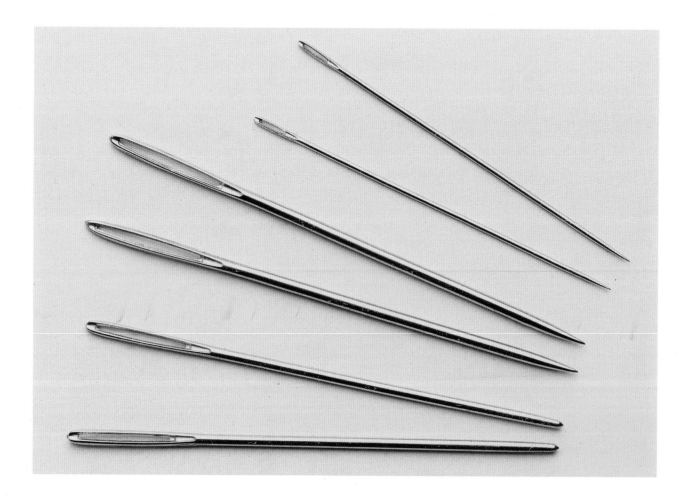

Shadow work requires the use of fine embroidery threads to make shadows within a design. For this you will need fine crewel embroidery needles, size 9 or 10 (the finer the needle the better, as this will help achieve a more refined effect).

Mountmellick and textural surfaces are all about creating texture, giving the design a three-dimensional, relief look. The needles need to be sufficiently large to take the thickness and weight of the strong soft cotton threads used: a size 5 crewel embroidery needle or chenille needles, sizes 20–24. The latter resemble tapestry needles, having a large eye, but they also have a point to take the threads through the strong fabric.

Ayrshire or fine whitework is worked on a very fine linen fabric in fine detail, therefore requiring a fine needle. Crewel embroidery needles are used, possibly a 9, 10 or even a size 12.

Needle cleaner

This is used to clean needles and keep them sharp when they get sticky so that they glide through the fabric, especially when working intensely with the finer techniques. The needle cleaner is filled with emery powder or iron filings.

Left Needles

Right Needle cleaners. Courtesy of the Royal School of Needlework.

Scissors

Two types of scissors are used for whitework. The first, a good sharp pair of fine pointed scissors to help cut and trim fraying ends, is important in cutwork and drawn thread work. The second pair, which has one rounded blade, is helpful in shadow appliqué and fine whitework, where there are layers of fabrics and only one layer is to be cut.

Above Scissors

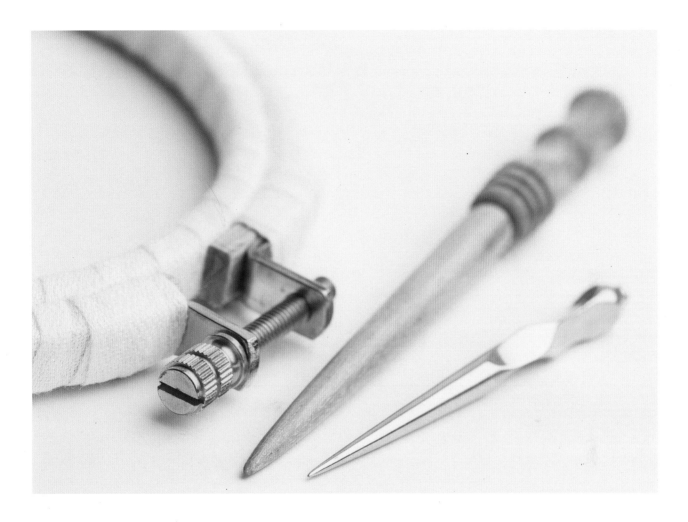

Stiletto

A stiletto looks like a large needle without an eye and is used for making small holes in firm, lightweight, closely woven fine fabric, such as the cottons or linens used for broderie anglaise or Ayrshire whitework.

Frame

Whitework needs to be worked on a frame, whether this is a ring frame or a slate frame. The frame helps keep the correct tension on the fabric that is being embroidered, especially if the fabric is cut. It is also important to keep the frame absolutely clean. If using a ring frame, bind both rings with white fine cotton strips. This will help stop ring frame marks and keep the embroidery immaculate. When putting whitework into a ring frame, place tissue paper on top of the fabric and place the work into the ring frame. Tear away the area of tissue paper that covers the part of the design that is to be worked. On a slate frame, use white cotton sheets or tissue paper around the rollers, and always keep work covered, except for the area that is being embroidered.

CHAPTER 2
Materials and threads

This section gives suitable fabrics and threads for each whitework technique, plus advice on how to transfer a design onto fabric before starting work.

Broderie anglaise

Materials
Choose a firm, lightweight, closely woven fine fabric, such as cotton and, occasionally, linen.

- White cambric
- Fine cotton lawn
- Very fine linen
- Muslin

Threads
The working thread should match the fabric used in colour, texture and quality, and the thickness of the thread should be the same as the thickness of the yarn warp and weft.

- Stranded cotton
- Coton à broder
- Floche à broder

Transferring a design
Use a light box and a sharp blue pencil to trace the design onto the fabric.

Richelieu and cutwork

Materials
Choose linen that is strong, stiff and firm, white or unbleached, and with a close weave, otherwise the material will fray after the spaces are cut.

Threads
The working thread should equal the fabric used in texture and quality, and can be any colour, although the beauty of this work lies in its design and technique. The thickness of the thread should match the thickness of the yarn warp and weft, but a thicker thread can be used for padding.

- Linen thread
- Cotton thread

- Mercerized cotton thread
- Stranded cotton
- Coton à broder
- Floche à broder

Transferring a design
Use a light box and a sharp blue pencil to trace the design onto the fabric.

Drawn thread work

Materials
Use a good quality evenweave fabric, one from which the threads of the fabric can be easily withdrawn. The weave chosen should not be too dense, but visible enough to make it possible to count the threads and with threads strong enough for them to be withdrawn without snapping.

- Linen
- Linen-look synthetics
- Linen blends
- Cotton
- Heavy silks
- Hessian

Threads
The working thread for decoration should on the whole be equal in quality to that of the threads of the fabric, though it may be coarser in size. Use a finer thread for buttonholing and hem stitching.

- Linen threads
- Cotton perlé threads
- Coton à broder
- Danish flower threads
- Crochet cottons
- Novelty threads, such as ribbons or braids

Transferring a design
Start by working out the design on graph or squared paper. Count the border patterns required, marking their position by tacking (basting) along the grain lines of the fabric.

Pulled work

Materials

The fabric must be an evenweave type, where the thread count per inch or centimetre on both warp and weft is equal. It should be slightly open, as a too closely woven fabric will look puckered when pulled work stitches are used on it. The more open the fabric, the lacier the effect.

- Linen
- Linen scrim
- Muslin
- Selected cottons

Threads

The working thread should be of the same colour, texture and thickness as the thread of the fabric. Finer threads may also be used, as the aim of pulled work is to show the different patterns that are produced within the fabric by the different stitches.

- Linen threads
- Coton à broder
- Danish flower thread
- Crochet cottons

Card A	Card B	Card C

Card A

Lightweight Irish linen
Mediumweight Irish linen
Zweigart Edinburgh linen, 36 count
Zweigart Belfast linen, 32 count
Zweigart Jazlyn linen, 28 count
Zweigart Annabelle linen, 28 count
Zweigart Brittney linen, 28 count
Zweigart Quaker cloth, Bantry
    linen, 28 count
Zweigart Cashel linen, 28 count
Zweigart Linda linen, 27 count
Zweigart Lugana linen, 25 count
Zweigart Dublin linen, 25 count

Card B

Organza
Organdie
Satin jeans fabric (Mountmellick)
Suedette
Antique white linen, 60 count
Cream linen, 50 count
Beige linen, 30 count
Fine antique white linen, 30 count
Cream linen, 30 count
Beige/cream linen, 25 count
White linen, 25 count
Pale beige linen, 22 count

Card C

Kitchen roll
Tablecloth paper
Handmade petal paper
Japanese paper
Woven paper
Calico
Natural-coloured heavy cotton
Fine natural silk
Silk noil
Straw fabric
Hessian
Coarse hessian

Transferring a design

Draw the design on tissue paper, marking the centre lines of the design. Place the tissue paper on the evenweave fabric, matching the centre lines, and tack (baste) through all the lines of the design, securing the threads at the start and the end. Finally, pull away the tissue paper to leave the tacking (basting) lines.

Shadow work

Materials

Choose a transparent or semi-transparent fabric, pale and delicate in colour, so that the shadow of the stitch shows through.

- Organdie
- Organza
- Muslin
- Any lightweight semi-transparent fabric

Threads

Use fine thread – either self-coloured, showing a shadow only, or coloured – bearing in mind that the colours are softened down as closed herringbone stitch is worked on the wrong side of the fabric.

Transferring a design

Draw the mirror image of the design on the wrong side of the fabric, as closed herringbone stitch will be worked from the back of the work. This is especially important to note if the design contains lettering.

Mountmellick and textural surfaces

Materials

Heavy cotton satin, also known as 'jeans' fabric, is used. This has a satin weave on the right side and a plain weave on the wrong side.

Threads

Traditional Mountmellick thread is matt white cotton, similar to crochet or knitting cotton rather than embroidery thread. Different thicknesses of cotton can be used to vary the texture of the design.

- Traditional Mountmellick thread
- Crochet cotton
- Knitting cotton
- Soft cotton

Transferring a design

It may be possible to draw the design on the fabric with the aid of a light box, by placing the design on the light box, covering it with the fabric and tracing through. Alternatively, use the traditional prick and pounce method.

Ayrshire and fine whitework

Materials

Use a firm, lightweight, closely woven fine fabric, such as cotton and, occasionally, linen.

- Cotton muslin
- Very fine linen
- Cambric

Threads

Traditionally, unmercerized cotton thread was used, with a matt surface, not a shiny one.

- Stranded cotton
- Coton à broder
- Floche à broder
- For finer detail, lace threads

Transferring a design

Use a light box and a sharp blue pencil to trace the design on the fabric.

Bondaweb (fusible webbing)

In addition to the fabrics and threads listed above, you may need to use Bondaweb for specific styles of whitework in order to stop fabrics fraying or to bond one fabric to another. Bondaweb is a web of fibre and glue bonded with a greaseproof paper. Iron the Bondaweb onto the fabric with the glue side facing the fabric and the paper side facing the iron. Remove the paper after ironing.

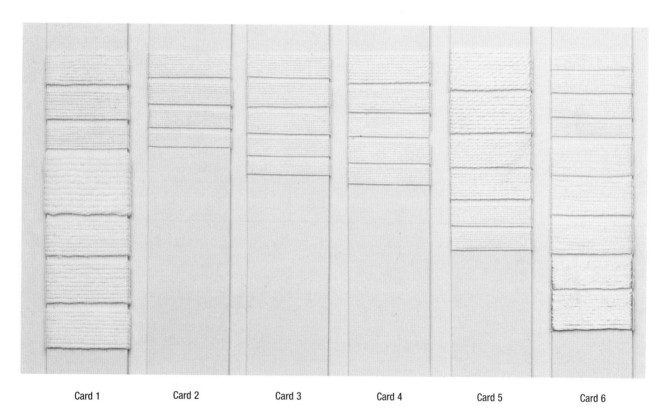

Card 1   Card 2   Card 3   Card 4   Card 5   Card 6

Card 1
Mountmellick no. 4
Mountmellick no. 3
Mountmellick no. 2
Coats Lyric 8/8
Coats Lyric 8/4
DMC soft cotton blanc
Anchor soft cotton no. 1

Card 2
DMC Cébélia no. 10
DMC Cordonnet Special no. 5
DMC Cordonnet Special no. 20
DMC Cordonnet Special no. 40

Card 3
Coats Eldorado
Coats Aida no. 5
Coats Aida no. 10
Coats Aida no. 20
Coats Aida no. 30

Card 4
DMC Petra no. 5
DMC Babylo 10/8
DMC Babylo 20/12
Coats Floretta no. 10, Col. 4400
Coats Floretta no. 20, Col. 4400

Card 5
Coats cotton perlé no. 3, Col. 1
DMC cotton perlé no. 3, Col. blanc
Coats cotton perlé no. 5, Col. 1
DMC cotton perlé no. 5, Col. blanc
Coats cotton perlé no. 8, Col. 1
DMC cotton perlé no. 8, Col. blanc

Card 6
DMC coton floche à broder
DMC coton à broder no.16, Col. blanc
Anchor coton à broder no. 16, Col. 1
Anchor coton à broder no. 30, Col. 1
Anchor stranded cotton, Col. 1
DMC stranded cotton, Col. B5200
DMC stranded cotton, Col. blanc
Anchor Marlitt, Col. 800
DMC rayon floss, Col. B5200

CHAPTER 3

Broderie anglaise

Broderie anglaise border
Sample border of broderie anglaise worked on
very fine cotton muslin, showing small round
and teardrop-shaped eyelets.

History

Broderie anglaise is simply the French term for 'English embroidery'. According to one school of thought, the technique is claimed to have developed from Czechoslovakian peasant embroidery and was brought to England in the ninth century. There are other ideas on the evolution of broderie anglaise, however. Appearing in the mid-1800s, it may have evolved from Ayrshire embroidery or was developed in its own right but at the same time.

If broderie anglaise originated in Ayrshire, it may be concluded that eyelets replaced the intricate fillings typical of the Ayrshire style. Some of the satin-stitched motifs of Ayrshire continued to be used, but were eventually replaced by eyelets. Thus the designs became more rhythmic and repetitive as they were worked along numerous cotton borders.

The other possibility, that broderie anglaise came into being around the same time as Ayrshire, suggests that this dominantly eyeleted work copied and incorporated satin stitch and larger cutwork motifs from Ayrshire. Original or earlier styles of broderie anglaise demonstrate designs such as flowers, leaves and stems worked entirely in eyelets. Possibly, Ayrshire devices may have influenced broderie anglaise and the two styles were combined.

These ornate patterns were utilized along the collars, cuffs and hems of garments or along the borders of other cotton or linen household items. Broderie anglaise is thought to have become more popular than Ayrshire embroidery some time around 1860, when fashions changed. It is not well documented, but one reason might be that it was simpler and quicker to execute. Broderie anglaise was worked on a heavier weight of cotton than the finer Ayrshire grounds. This fact alone would have made it more durable for commonplace domestic uses and therefore more popular with the working and middle classes.

The rhythm and repetition of the eyelet patterns made broderie anglaise perfect for reproduction by machine, and from 1870 broderie anglaise was produced on a far greater scale.

Worked both by hand and more so by machine, broderie anglaise is still popular today and can be found mainly on bedlinen, baby items and some ladies' fashions.

Broderie anglaise stitches

Stiletto eyelets

As the name suggests, these eyelets, measuring less than 5mm (¼in) in diameter, are made with a stiletto.

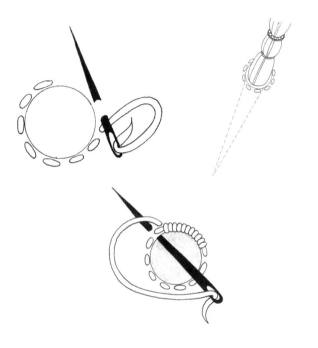

Method

1. Begin by marking each small eyelet with a dot.
2. Run a small running stitch around the dot or position for the eyelet.
3. Pierce the dot or position for the eyelet with a stiletto, making a hole.
4. Oversew the edge of the hole, bringing the needle up just outside the running stitch and down into the hole.
5. Repeat, keeping the stitches very close to one another, and work around the circle until you are back at the beginning again.

Hints and tips

When starting the eyelet, leave a trail of thread. This can be threaded through the back when finished, along with the finishing thread.

If working a series of eyelets, it is possible to trail the thread on the back from eyelet to eyelet, as long as they are close to each other and the thread does not trail under the eyelets themselves.

Cut eyelets

Eyelets larger than 5mm (¼in) in diameter are cut.

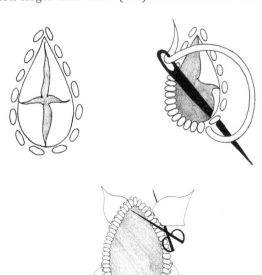

Method

1. Work a running stitch around the eyelet.
2. Cut the eyelet both vertically and horizontally, cutting from the middle.
3. Fold back the four points of excess fabric and bring the needle up ready for oversewing just outside the running stitch.
4. Take the needle down into the hole and repeat all around the eyelet.
5. When finished, turn to the back of the work and cut away any excess fabric.

Hints and tips

See stiletto eyelets, above.

Creative broderie anglaise samples

Tufted eyelets
Small eyelets, less than 5mm (¼in) in diameter, are worked on natural linen fabric with no. 16 coton à broder thread. The eyelets are then mounted on acrylic fur fabric, which is pulled through them to create a fine, misty effect.

Cut paper eyelets
These cut eyelets are worked on handmade natural paper: two layers of paper are first glued together with Bondaweb (fusible webbing), and each cut circle is drawn around a small coin, and then slashed with a fine pair of scissors, first into quarters and then eighths, up to the circle line. Next, each triangle is folded back onto the circle line, and tacked (basted) around with no. 16 coton à broder thread to hold back the triangle of paper on the front of the work.

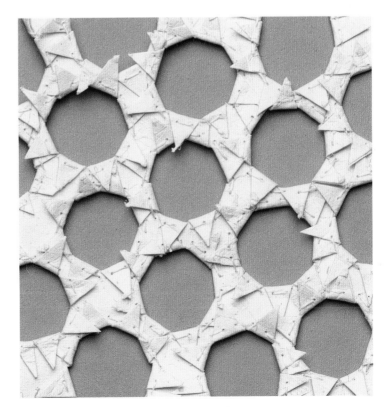

Above:

Jelly Fish

Sally Saunders

Broderie anglaise eyelets and cutwork edges
are worked on layers of cotton fabric built on
top of one another, with the final layer padded
to give depth and texture.

Left:

Moon Daisy

Nicola Jarvis

The 'Moon Daisy' is worked on deck chair cotton
canvas and painted with fabric paint. Petal
markings, satin stitch circles and large eyelets
have been worked in various thicknesses of
thread, including stranded cotton, buttonhole
thread and Gütermann sewing thread.

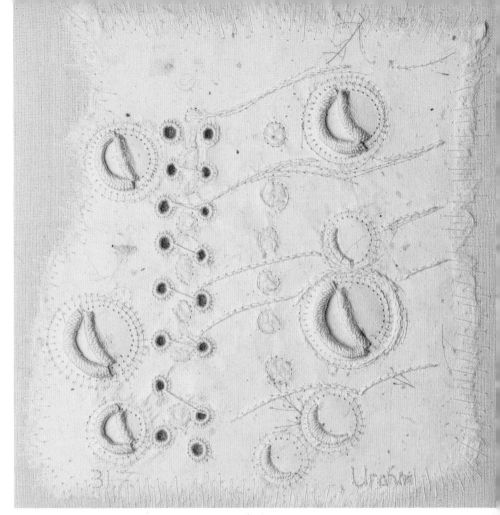

Urchin
Design: Nicola Jarvis
Embroidery: Tracy A Franklin
Handmade seed paper was torn and applied
to calico. Eyelets and surface stitching were
worked in hand-dyed perlé cottons and
natural-coloured machine sewing thread.
Some parts of the paper have been wetted
and then textured by manipulating the
paper, causing it to pucker slightly.

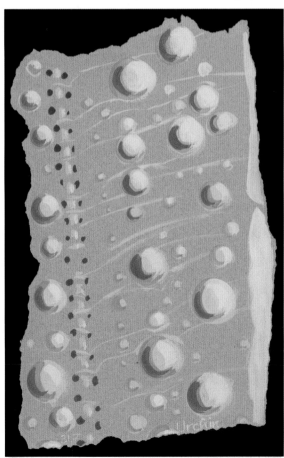

CHAPTER 4

Richelieu and cutwork

History

Richelieu cutwork embroidery has its origins in 16th-century Italy, where it was known as Venetian lace. Cardinal Richelieu was principal minister to Louis XIII and he desired that France should become a self-sufficient state. Thus, among his reforms he welcomed many Italian lacemakers to teach the intricate cutwork technique to the natives. France later became renowned for this fine embroidery.

The technique was used to embroider motifs that were mostly floral and organic. Richelieu cutwork typically displays cut-away shapes, the edges of which are connected by buttonhole bars decorated with picots.

Other forms of the Richelieu technique include Renaissance embroidery and the original Venetian embroidery. The former resembles Richelieu in that it has supporting bars worked in buttonhole stitch. The buttonhole stitch is executed over a single thread and is of a uniform size throughout the design. However, unlike Richelieu, Renaissance embroidery incorporates satin stitch fillings in areas adjacent to the cutwork.

In contrast to Richelieu, Venetian embroidery demonstrates a profusion of surface embroidery. The outlines surrounding the cut areas are heavily padded and become a focal point of the design.

Cutwork was originally executed on a linen ground. Areas were literally cut away once the design lines had been worked in buttonhole stitch. Nuns were thought to have executed the majority of early Richelieu cutwork, though outworkers were employed to assist in the production of ecclesiastical vestments and linens.

Richelieu cutwork was produced by machine as well as by hand in the 20th century. It can be seen today on home furnishings and selected women's wear.

Drawstring cutwork bag
This pretty bag is worked in Richelieu cutwork on linen and lined with saffron-coloured silk, drawn together with silk ribbon.

Richelieu and cutwork stitches

Buttonhole stitch

The looped edge makes this buttonhole stitch suitable for an edging, as the tight line of loops prevents fraying when the fabric is cut away. The running stitch helps to give a good strong edge and stops the fabric stretching too much.

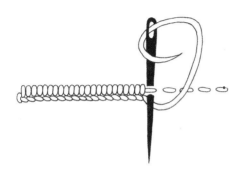

Method

1. Work a small running stitch on the ground fabric, just off the lower edge line.
2. Working from left to right, bring the thread up on the lower line and make a loop of thread on the surface of the fabric.
3. Insert the needle on the top line, which can be any width between 2 and 5mm (½ and ¼in), and bring it through on the lower line, up through the loop and *over* the working thread.
4. A long straight stitch is formed, with a looped edge on the lower line and the thread is then in place to begin the next stitch.

Hints and tips

When working buttonhole stitch, keep the stitches close together and taut. This is particularly important if cutting is intended.

When working buttonhole stitch, remember that the looped edge should be worked on the edge intended for cutting.

Buttonhole stitch picots

These picots can be worked either on detached buttonhole stitch or on buttonhole stitching that is connected to the ground fabric.

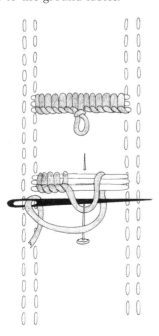

Method

1. Begin by working the buttonhole stitch from left to right, with the loops facing downwards.
2. Once halfway across the bar, insert a pin into the ground fabric at the position of the next buttonhole stitch.
3. The pin should be placed sticking out slightly, so that a well-shaped picot can be worked.
4. Take the thread around the pin and then back under the bar.
5. Next, take the needle *underneath* the loop of thread created by the pin and then *over* the working thread.
6. Pull tight and continue working the buttonhole stitch as before.

Hints and tips

Slightly exaggerate the intended length of the picot, as it will shrink in slightly when the pin is removed.

Keep the buttonhole stitches and picot as tight as possible when working, as they can unravel.

If there is no ground fabric to take a pin to, make a picot, then temporarily place the embroidery onto some cotton fabric to support it.

Crescent-shaped motifs with buttonhole bars

The bars of buttonhole are placed specifically to hold the crescent shape together and to keep the fabric strong. If the crescent shape is larger than 2.5cm (1in), it is advisable to add more buttonhole bars.

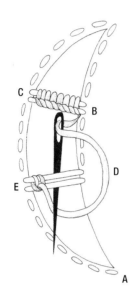

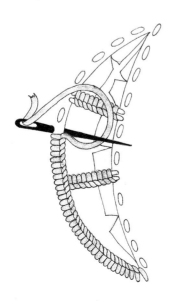

Method

1. Work a small running stitch just outside the design line to be cut, clockwise from point A around the shape until the position for the first bar to be worked, at point B.
2. At point B, throw a thread bar across to point C, where the needle enters the fabric close to the running stitch line.
3. Take the needle back to point B, where again it holds the fabric, then take it again to point C.
4. At point C, work detached buttonhole stitch from left to right, bringing the needle up below the bar, forming a loose loop of thread, and then taking the needle underneath the bar from the top and up through the loop.
5. Work buttonhole stitch back to point B, and then continue the running stitch to point D.
6. As before, work a buttonhole bar from point D to point E and back again, and then take the running stitch to point A at the beginning.
7. At this stage, cut the fabric within the crescent shape and underneath the bars right down the middle and slash two to three times at each side, up against the design line, so that it can be folded back easily.
8. Work buttonhole stitch again over this folded edge, starting at point A.
9. Bring the needle up inside the crescent shape, forming a loop.
10. Take the needle back into the fabric, over the running stitch line, and then back up through the loop and *over* the working thread.
11. Continue the buttonhole stitch around the crescent and back to point A.
12. Afterwards, cut any surplus fabric from the back.

Hints and tips

When throwing the bars of thread for buttonhole stitch, make sure that they are taut, as the buttonhole stitch may stretch them, causing them to become loose.

When cutting the fabric, always start cutting carefully from the middle.

When working buttonhole stitch, remember that the looped edge should be worked on the edge intended for cutting.

Buttonhole stitch with bar, ladder work

As with the previous stitch, the bars of buttonhole have been placed deliberately to hold the shape together and to keep the fabric strong.

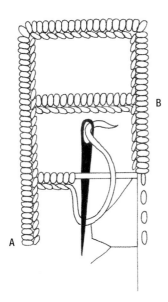

Method

1. Work a small running stitch just outside the design line to be cut.
2. Cut the fabric right down the middle and slash two to three times on each side, up against the design line, so that it can be folded back easily.
3. Work buttonhole stitch from point A over this folded edge, as follows.
4. Bring the needle up inside the cut area formed, creating a loop on top.
5. Take the needle back into the fabric over the running stitch line, and then back up through the loop and *over* the working thread.
6. Continue the buttonhole stitch to point B, which is the position of the first cross bar.
7. At point B, throw a thread bar across to the opposite side and secure it.
8. Returning back to point B, work detached buttonhole stitch from left to right, bringing the needle up below the bar, forming a loose loop of thread, and then taking the needle underneath the bar from the top and coming up through the loop, as shown.
9. Continue buttonholing down the shape to the next cross bar.
10. Once all the stitching is complete, trim any surplus fabric from the back.

Hints and tips

When throwing the bars of thread ready to be buttonholed, make sure that they are taut, as the buttonhole stitch may stretch them, causing them to become loose. If they become too tight, however, they may pull the cut shape out of place.

When trimming the fabric, always cut carefully from the middle first. When working buttonhole stitch, remember that the looped edge should be worked on the edge intended for cutting.

Creative Richelieu samples

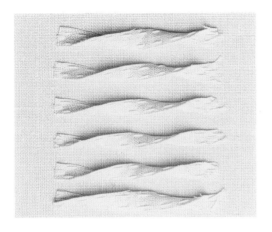

Twisted bars

Bond a sample piece of the ground fabric with Bondaweb (fusible webbing) to prevent fraying. Take the sample piece of fabric and, using fine crochet cotton, work a pair of running stitch lines down the grain of the fabric, setting them approximately 5–6mm (¼in) apart and leaving the threads unsecured. Cut out a strip of linen from between the lines and apply it to the ground fabric by twisting it slightly and holding both left and right edges with three stitches. Work more strips of linen in the same way and apply to the ground fabric, laying them parallel and twisting the same number of times and the same way.

Cut and flipped

This sample is worked on two layers of linen fabric, bonded together with Bondaweb for stability. A series of long V-shapes are cut, with the inner part folded back on itself. Using coton à broder thread, work running stitches in a long V shape across the linen. Using sharp scissors, cut the V shape inside the running stitch, leaving it uncut at the widest part. Fold the V shape back on itself and hold it down with a small stitch. Work a buttonhole bar over the small stitch by throwing three long stitches over the end of the V and buttonholing over them.

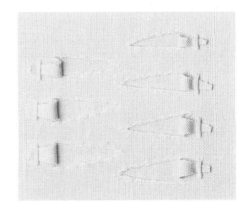

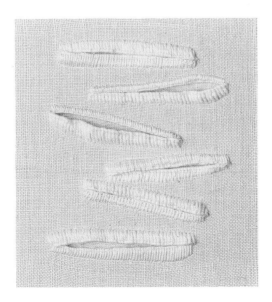

Slashed and buttonholed

This sample is again worked on two layers of firm linen, bonded together with Bondaweb. Slash the linen by cutting with sharp scissors. Using a combination of different thread types – soft cotton, coton à broder and Aida crochet cotton – work buttonhole stitch along both edges. Some edges may be worked over twice or even three times to make the effect heavier and slightly puckered.

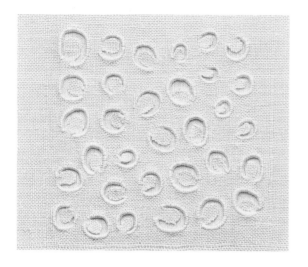

Incomplete cut eyelets

This sample is worked on two layers of firm linen, bonded together with Bondaweb (fusible webbing). Crochet cotton is used to create incomplete eyelets by first working a line of small running stitches in an almost complete circle. Using sharp scissors, the eyelets are cut within the running stitch, leaving the fabric attached where the stitching stops. Oversew the edge of the cut fabric and the running stitch, bringing the needle up behind the running stitch and down into the eyelet. Some eyelets are oversewn twice or three times to give them a slightly padded look, and these are evenly spread within the square.

Big circular cut eyelets

These cut eyelets are worked on two layers of firm linen, bonded together with Bondaweb. The threads used are crochet cotton and a few strands of stranded cotton, combined in the needle. Begin by working a running stitch circle, then cut away the central part of the circle. Oversew the edge of the circle and the running stitch by bringing the needle up behind the stitches and down into the hole. Some circles are worked over twice or three times and the ends of the threads are left unfinished on the surface. Work the circles very close together, so that there is little of the linen ground fabric showing.

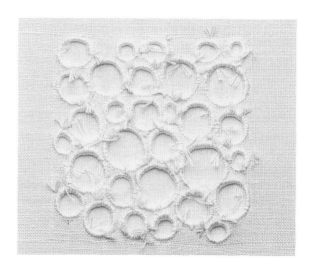

Cut fabric circles

The ground fabric is bonded with Bondaweb to prevent fraying. On a separate piece of the ground fabric, draw circles around a small coin and cut them from the fabric. Using coton à broder, work small running stitches close to the edge of each cut circle. Tie the ends of the threads on the bonded side of the circle, slightly pulling the stitches so that they cup the circles. Place the cut-out circles on the ground fabric, and anchor each in the centre with three small straight stitches.

Puckered cut flowers

This sample requires a template of a simple flower with five petals. Cut the shape out of card and use it to draw the design on the right side of a piece of the same fabric as the ground fabric, bonded with Bondaweb (fusible webbing) to prevent fraying. Draw around the flower shape very lightly with a sharp pencil and repeat to make a pattern of overlapping shapes. Other than the top shapes, avoid drawing round the whole shape each time; draw only up to the previous shape. Cut out selected areas on the drawn line without cutting anything completely. Place on the ground fabric and backstitch using fine crochet cotton along the lines that are visible, slightly manipulating the fabric so that it becomes more three-dimensional.

Cut woven bars

This sample has been heavily embroidered with fine crochet cotton and a soft cotton thread. Two layers of firm linen are bonded together using Bondaweb, and three large shapes are drawn on top. Begin by working running stitch contour lines on the outside of the shapes to give extra support. Work buttonhole stitch around each shape, with horizontal bars thrown across close together. Cut away the areas of ground cloth within the buttonhole stitching, being careful not to cut the bars. Using a combination of soft cotton and fine crochet cotton in the needle, weave in and out of the bars, leaving the ends of the threads unfinished.

Slashed fabric buttonhole bars

This cutwork sample is worked on one layer of the linen fabric only. It is slashed or cut vertically up the sample six or seven times and then buttonholed, using Aida crochet thread to secure the ground fabric vertically only at this stage. The sample is worked quite crudely, so the lines of buttonhole stitch are not necessarily parallel with each other and may cross. Horizontal buttonhole bars are then worked over the vertical slashed areas, pulling it back together. The buttonhole bars are worked quite heavily, building on what has already been worked.

Left:
Cut paper
Catherine Howard
Paper cut and manipulated into
flower shapes.

Right:
Daisies
Florence Collingwood
Cut daisies applied with a
centre of beads and trailing
stems, accompanied by text.

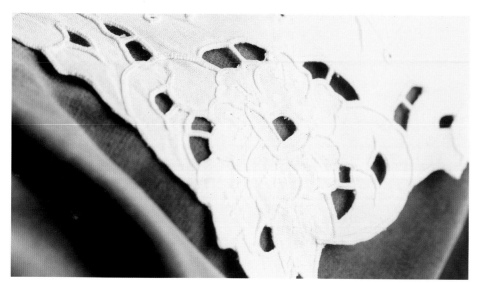

Left:
Cutwork traycloth
This traycloth has been created
using buttonhole stitch, buttonhole
bars and surface embroidery.

Cutwork fringe
Sally Saunders
This sample piece of cutwork is worked on fine
linen fabric with white stranded cotton.

The Common Daisies

Nicola Jarvis

These simple daisy flowers were worked in the traditional Richelieu technique, but the usual combination of linen fabric and white thread has been replaced by a chiffon ground, with embroidery executed in strips of plastic.

Running stitch was worked around the daisy petals and then buttonhole stitch was worked over this on the central daisy. Traditionally, the running stitches acted as padding for the buttonhole stitch. However, in this design the artist has chosen to leave the padding exposed. It thus becomes a decorative device to mark out the petal shapes. The centre of each daisy is worked with a circle of satin stitch.

The chiffon background fabric was cut away inside the petals of the buttonholed daisy. In the rest of the design, the chiffon remains uncut, apart from the fringe at the bottom of the daisy cluster.

In between the plastic buttonhole and running stitches, vintage glass beads have been attached. The artist wanted to juxtapose the contemporary material of plastic with antique glass to create an interesting tension. The design was appliquéd to a natural linen backing.

Above:

Panel

Amanda Clayton

Dense areas of darning stitches in silk floss thread cover this sheer silk fabric, with areas exposed in between trailing lines.

Left:

Haiku

Margaret Clementson

Cutwork flowers are embroidered on silk crepe, buttonholed with silk embroidery thread. The embroidery is accompanied with supporting sketches, photographs and threads to show its development from the initial concept.

CHAPTER 5

Drawn thread work

History

When the tomb of St Cuthbert was opened at Durham Cathedral in the 12th century, a monk recorded that the saint's shroud was edged with an inch-long fringe and surmounted by a border 'worked upon threads'. It may be surmised that this border might have been a very early example of drawn thread work.

This filigree technique is considered by many to be a type of needle-made lace. It was traditionally created on a linen ground by removing certain warp and weft threads. The remaining threads and spaces were embellished with decorative stitch patterns and needle-weaving to strengthen the open structures.

Examples of drawn thread work that date back to the 15th century have been found in Italy. Bedcovers, curtains and tablecloths, many belonging to the nobility of Bologna, were decorated with drawn thread borders. Further south, the drawn thread work of Sicily became renowned for its excellence. Geometric forms from Arabian culture influenced the embroidered patterns of this area.

The elaborate drawn thread work from Italy came to be known as *reticella*. Its popularity spread throughout Europe during the 15th and 16th centuries. Lacemakers began cutting holes in the fabric ground instead of drawing out the threads. They then filled the open holes with stitches that literally extended into the empty spaces or air. Thus, this development became known as *punto in aria*, which literally means 'stitch in the air'.

Reticella was much admired by John Ruskin, who introduced the designs to the linen workers in the Lake District, England, where it became known as Ruskin lace.

Booklets were printed with details of motifs and designs for drawn thread work. Some of the earliest examples are from Germany, one of these being a booklet printed in Zwichau in 1525 and another printed in Cologne and dated 1527.

The ornate style of drawn thread work remained in existence until a simpler technique became popular in the 19th century. This was used for border motifs on household items, including tablecloths, linen bedclothes, curtains, underwear, handkerchiefs and aprons.

Drawn thread work continues to be executed today by amateur and professional hand embroiderers.

Drawn thread tablecloth
Threads have been withdrawn from a piece of fine white linen to create the borders and motifs on this tablecloth. Embroidery including interlacing and needleweaving complete the intricate effect.

Drawn thread work stitches

Drawing out threads

Drawn thread work is best worked on an evenweave fabric, in which the number of both warp and weft threads per inch is the same each way.

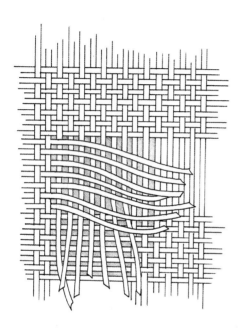

Method

1. Mark out a border for decoration. Working from the centre of the border, lift one of the long threads up with a tapestry needle and snip through it carefully.
2. Tease the cut thread up and out from the crossing threads, up to the marked destination one way, and then repeat until you have removed the other threads that are to be withdrawn to that edge.
3. Return to the centre of the border and withdraw the other half of the cut threads in the opposite direction in the same way.

Hints and tips

It is important to mark out the areas from which the threads of the fabric are to be withdrawn, using tacking (basting) stitches.

It is also important that the threads remaining in the withdrawn thread areas are of the correct number for the pattern to be worked (see pages 50–55)

When teasing out the threads, pull only *one* thread out at a time, and only a little at a time.

When nearing the edge of the fabric, be very careful not to accidentally pull out the full thread. Hold the remaining thread in place to ensure that this does not happen and that the thread only pulls to the line intended.

Reweaving

This secures the edge, ready for the design to be worked.

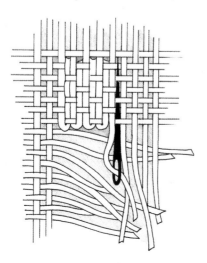

Method

1. Once the threads have been withdrawn up to the design line, trim them all down to a reasonable length, leaving sufficient to be able to thread a needle and reweave.
2. Using a tapestry needle, take each thread in turn and weave it back into the fabric along the side it came from.

Hints and tips

If reweaving part of the outer border, it may be best to reweave the threads back to the outer edge of the evenweave fabric, as this may look more presentable.

If the border is part of the central design and the end of the border is to be buttonholed, then it may be necessary only to reweave the threads back two to three threads of the fabric, leaving the ends uncut until the buttonholing has been worked.

Buttonhole stitch after reweaving

To secure the ends of the withdrawn threads, buttonhole stitch can be worked after the threads have been woven back over two to three threads into the evenweave fabric. Leave the tails uncut until the buttonhole stitch has been worked.

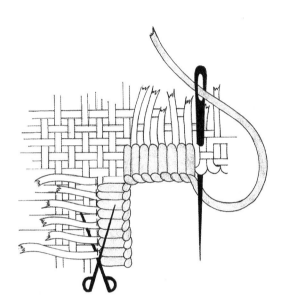

Method

1. Work buttonhole stitch around the two outer edges of a corner where two borders meet, using a thread slightly finer than the thread of the fabric and a pointed embroidery needle. To start, secure the thread where it will not be seen, ready to work left to right, and bring it up on the edge to be stitched.
2. Create a loop on the surface, and take the needle down through the front of the fabric, two to three threads from the edge, depending on the count of the fabric.
3. Bring the needle up from *underneath* and through the loop *over* the working thread.
4. Pull the stitch firmly and continue to buttonhole very closely to make the edge secure.
5. The corners can be worked one of two ways, depending on the effect to be achieved, the strength of the fabric and the working area itself.
6. For the first type, work as far up to the corner as possible, and turn the corner at right angles to continue, as shown. This corner is tidier and works well on strong fabric.
7. Alternatively, work as far up to the corner as possible and then fan out the buttonhole stitches right into the corner, so that it becomes parallel with the thread, ready to work up the other side of the corner. This method is more secure, but can look less attractive.
8. Finally, the rewoven threads of the fabric need to be cut. One at a time, slightly over-pull the thread and, using sharp scissors, cut neatly so that the thread shrinks back out of sight underneath the buttonhole stitch.

Hints and tips

If you are working a very open design on a fine evenweave fabric, it is important to take into account how reweaving and buttonhole stitch will affect the overall design. The work needs to be strong and secure to prevent any fraying and weak areas.

As this buttonhole stitch is always quite prominent within a design, make sure that the working thread is fresh and not 'tired-looking'.

Hemstitching

The majority of drawn thread borders are hemstitched along both edges. This has the function of securing the hem, strengthening the border and tying the loose threads into groups in order to work decorative patterns.

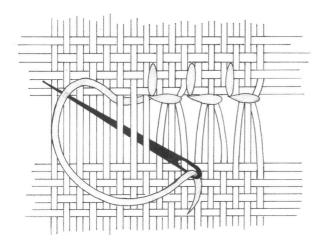

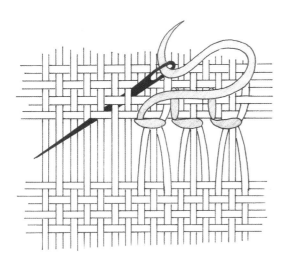

Method

1. Before working the hem stitching, it is important to plan out in advance the border patterns that are to be worked, as they are all grouped in different multiples and this may determine whether they are grouped in twos, threes or fours.
2. Hemstitch is worked from right to left, using a thread of the same thickness as the threads of the evenweave fabric. Using a tapestry needle (to prevent splitting of threads), secure the thread and bring the needle up from behind, three threads in front.
3. Take the needle and thread back around this group of three threads and up again from behind in the same place, and then pull the group of threads together.
4. Take the needle into the fabric vertically over two threads, as shown below left.
5. Bring the needle up again three threads in front, ready to start the next stitch.

Hints and tips

It is possible to use different thicknesses and types of threads for hemstitching, depending on the effect that is to be created.

When hemstitching the other side of the border, group threads in the same way, so that bunches of threads are ready to be decorated; alternatively, they can be bunched so that a zigzag effect occurs, especially if grouping in twos or fours.

A simple interlaced border

Any type of thread or yarn, even ribbon, can be used to produce this interlaced border.

Method

1. Work from right to left. Using a tapestry needle, secure the working thread at the end of the border, ready to start in the middle.
2. Take the needle over the first two groups of threads.
3. Bring the needle back *under* the second group of threads *only* and *over* the first group.
4. Using the needle, push the first group of threads forward in front of the second, pulling the working thread so it becomes straight.
5. The needle and thread are then in position, ready to start interlacing again.

Hints and tips

Once the border has been worked, use a pin to tweak and straighten out the central line.

If the border is wide, it is possible to work a double interlaced border, in which four groups of threads are intertwined, or to work two lines of interlacing within the same border.

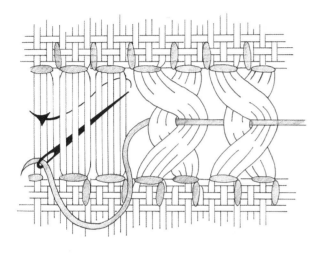

Simple knotted border

Variations of this stitch can be worked in lines or in a zigzag formation.

Method

1. Work from right to left, using a tapestry needle. Secure the working thread at the end of the border, ready to start in the middle.
2. Form a loop of thread over the surface of the border to be worked.
3. Take the needle down *behind* the loop of thread, and *underneath* three groups of threads.
4. Bring the needle *up* after the third group and *up* through the loop of thread.
5. Pull the groups of threads firmly together within the knot.
6. The needle and thread are then in position ready to repeat the process.

Hints and tips

When pulling the knot, make sure that the thread is taut from the previous knot so that there is something secure to pull against.

The actual knot may have to be tugged right and left slightly to tighten it firmly.

Choose a thread or yarn that will stay held as a knot and will not slip or loosen.

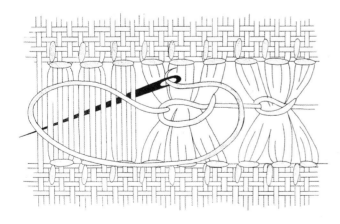

Overcast bar

The method shown below is the most straightforward. Other variations of overcasting or wrapping can be worked, however, including pulling the groups of threads together both at the top and the bottom so that the whole appearance becomes zigzagged instead of straight.

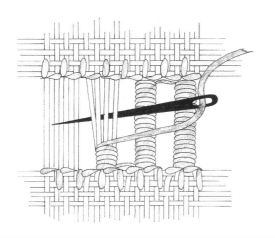

Method

1. Work from right to left, using a tapestry needle. Begin by trailing the tail end of the working thread parallel over the groups of threads to be wrapped.
2. Start wrapping with the working thread around the groups of threads, sealing in the tail end and making sure that each stitch is firm and taut.
3. Once the first group of threads has been completely wrapped, pass the thread under to the next bunch of threads.
4. Continue wrapping each group of threads in turn, working upwards, across, downwards, across, upwards and so on.

Hints and tips

If a new thread needs to be attached, trail the remaining working thread over the next group of threads to be wrapped along with new thread. Begin wrapping, sealing in both tail ends.

Simple weaving

The simple weaving shown below can be varied by working over more groups of threads, perhaps in blocks and stepped, and with different colours.

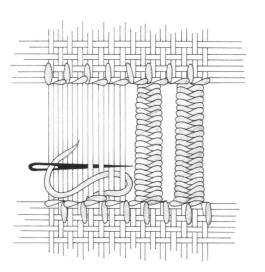

Method

1. Work from right to left, using a tapestry needle. Begin by trailing the tail end of the working thread parallel over the groups of threads to be woven, as when working an overcast bar.
2. Start weaving with the working thread between two groups of threads by coming up in the middle of the two groups and back over and under one group. Bring the thread up in the middle again and forward and under one group, continuously moving in a figure-of-eight and sealing in the tail end as you go.
3. Pass the thread to the next two groups of threads to be woven by coming up again in between the two groups. Work as before.
4. Continue weaving, working upwards, across, downwards, across, upwards and so on.

Hints and tips

If a new thread needs to be attached, trail the remaining working thread over the groups of threads to be woven and lay with it the new thread. Seal in both tail ends, one with one group and one with the other group, so that the effect does not look lopsided.

Making a grid and withdrawing threads

As well as borders, complete grounds, backgrounds or individual motifs can be worked over withdrawn threads on evenweave fabric. The techniques are the same, but careful planning is necessary, as both warp and weft threads are withdrawn. The threads can be withdrawn as a grid to form open areas within a design combined with of solid areas.

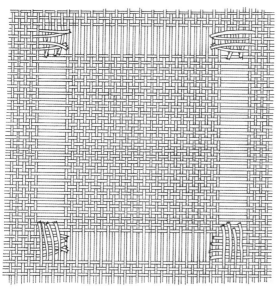

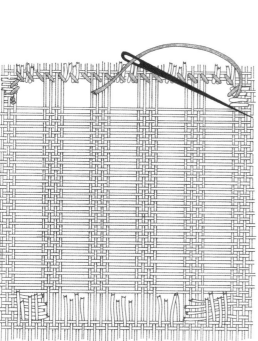

Method

1. Mark out the grid boundaries with tacking (basting) stitches, defining the overall size and the count to be withdrawn.
2. Begin withdrawing the border threads first of all, cutting from the middle and withdrawing up to the boundaries.
3. Next, withdraw the vertical threads by withdrawing four threads and leaving four continuously, again cutting from the middle.
4. To complete the grid, withdraw the horizontal threads in the same way.
5. When the whole grid is completed, reinforce all the outer edges with an overcast or buttonhole stitch, depending on the nature of the fabric, the design and the type of stitch to be worked within the grid.

Hints and tips

It is usual to make the grid in multiples of four, although other grid counts can be formed, depending on the stitch type to be worked over the top and the thread count of the evenweave fabric.

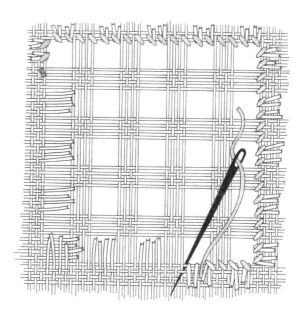

Knotted grid

This stitch is worked diagonally, connecting the groups of threads starting at the top left-hand side.

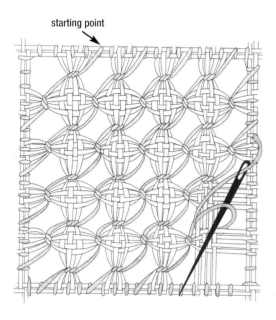

starting point

Method

1. The stitch is worked in steps, knotting the group of threads vertically then horizontally, working downwards, and then carrying the thread along the back to the next group of threads and working upwards, working horizontally, vertically, horizontally, and so on.
2. Using a tapestry needle, form a knot by taking the working thread over the group of threads to be tied and underneath, creating a loop around the threads.
3. Before the loop is pulled up, pass the needle with the thread through the loop, creating a knot.
4. Pull the knot, thus bunching together the group of threads.

Hints and tips

When pulling the knot, make sure that the thread is taut from the previous knot so that there is something secure to pull against.

The actual knot may have to be tugged right and left slightly to tighten it firmly.

Use a thread or yarn that will stay held as a knot and will not slip or loosen.

Overcast grid

This stitch is worked diagonally, the groups of threads being oversewn together, starting at the top left-hand side.

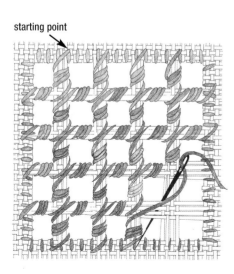

starting point

Method

1. Work the stitch in steps, oversewing the group of threads vertically then horizontally, working downwards, and then carrying the thread along the back to the next group of threads and working vertically upwards, then horizontally, vertically, horizontally, and so on.
2. Using a tapestry needle, take the working thread around the group of threads to cover sufficiently.
3. Make sure, when passing from one group to another, that a long slanted stitch appears on top at each intersection.

Hints and tips

It can be difficult to decide which way the needle needs to be working to ensure that a long slanted stitch appears on top at each intersection. It may therefore be easier to work each row diagonally, top right to bottom left, the right way round, turn the work upside down, then top right to bottom left, with the work upside down.

Looped stitch grid

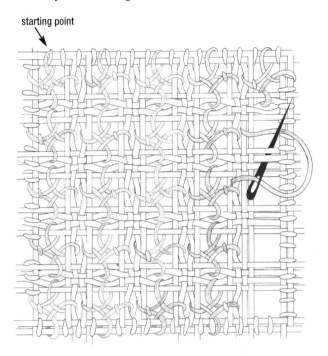

starting point

Method

1. The 'working' thread is secured at the top left corner of the grid at the side.
2. The needle is brought up at the edge and is worked anti-clockwise around a space by taking the needle over two threads of the grid at the bottom and bringing it up through the loop of thread.
3. The other two sides follow the same instruction.
4. On returning to the starting point, the process is different. Bring the needle up around the loop of thread and back down into the hole, so that the working thread has just worked a full loop and the whole loop stitch is complete.
5. Bring the needle up from underneath to start the next loop stitch.
6. Continue working the full row and then work all subsequent rows up and down the grid.

Hints and tips

With this stitch, it is quite important to note where the thread will need to appear in order to work the next loop and at the same time keep the overall effect consistent. Working in vertical rows allows the thread to be passed underneath the weave of the fabric to the same pattern each time.

Woven grid

This stitch is worked diagonally, the groups of threads being woven together, starting at the top left. It requires an even number of withdrawn threads.

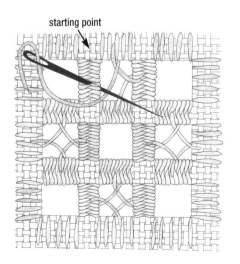

starting point

Method

1. The stitch is worked in steps. First, weave the group of threads vertically and then horizontally, working downwards.
2. Next, carry the thread along the back to the next group of threads and work upwards, working horizontally, vertically, horizontally, and so on.
3. Using a tapestry needle, bring the working thread up in the middle of the group of threads.
4. Begin weaving by taking the thread left and under the threads, up in the middle, and right under the threads, up in the middle, creating a figure-of-eight stitch, until the section is filled.

Hints and tips

The spaces can be filled with looped stitches or wheels (see pages 56–57).

Drawn thread corner

Open squares or corners are formed where two
borders of withdrawn threads meet. These corners
must be bound on all sides, either by overcasting,
needle weaving or buttonholed bars. The bars provide
a sturdy framework for decorative filling patterns
such as the ones described here.

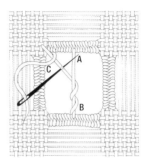
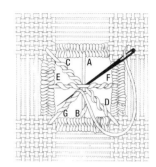

Spokes – woven wheel

This wheel can be worked either clockwise or anti-
clockwise over an odd number of spokes.

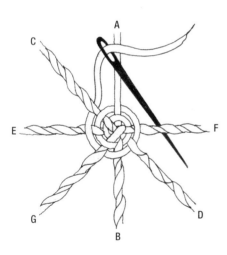

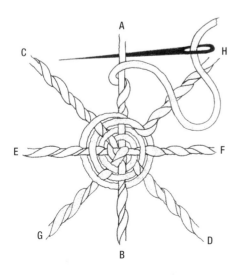

Method

1. Secure the 'working' thread and bring the needle
    up at A, in the middle of the bar.
2. Take the needle down at B and up from behind,
    winding the thread around the spoke to the
    centre. Keep a little tension on the thread.
3. Take the needle down at C and repeat the action
    by bringing the needle up from behind and
    winding to the centre.
4. Follow the sequence illustrated from C to D, D
    to E and so on till G, always working the spoke
    opposite to keep a good tension on the square.
5. After the G spoke has been worked, wind
    the thread back to the centre and pull the
    spokes together with a loop knot by taking the
    needle behind all the spokes and back through
    the loop formed.
6. It is important to note that a woven wheel can
    only be worked with an odd number of spokes,
    therefore at this stage spoke H is left out.
7. Begin weaving the thread over E and under C
    and continue in a clockwise direction until the
    desired size has been achieved.
8. Finish weaving after spoke A.
9. Bring the needle up at the edge of the web and
    create a spoke at H.
10. Wind the thread back along spoke H to the web.
    Take the needle behind the web and finish by
    winding the thread out along spoke A.

Hints and tips

Always try to maintain a good tension on the wheel,
as it can all too easily become limp.

Backstitched wheel

Like the woven wheel, the backstitched wheel can be worked clockwise or anti-clockwise, and its spokes are produced in exactly the same way as those for the woven wheel.

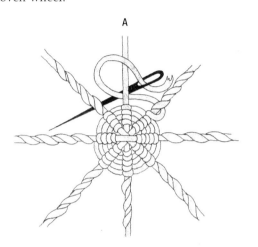

Method

1. In this case, unlike that of the woven wheel, it is not necessary to have an odd number of spokes, and therefore spoke H can be used.
2. As before, wind the thread back to the centre and pull the spokes together with a loop knot by taking the needle behind all the spokes and back through the loop formed.
3. Using a tapestry needle, begin working the back-stitched wheel by taking the thread *forward* and *underneath two* spokes, and then *back* over *one*, forming ridges where the spokes lie.
4. Keep working the wheel until the desired size has been achieved, stopping at spoke A.
5. Finish by winding the thread out along spoke A.

Hints and tips

Always try to maintain a good tension on the wheel, as it can all too easily become limp.

Knotted wheel

Again, the spokes for the knotted wheel are produced in exactly the same way as they were for the woven wheel and backstitched wheel. The number of spokes should be even, the quantity depending on the open size and the fineness of the threads used. As with the previous two, this wheel can be worked either clockwise or anti-clockwise.

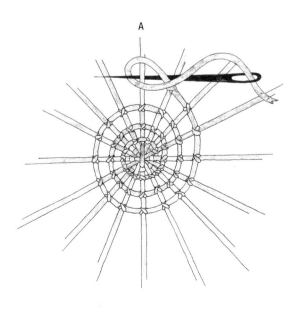

Method

1. As before, wind the thread of the last spoke back to the centre and pull the spokes together with a loop knot by taking the needle behind all the spokes and back through the loop formed.
2. Working around the wheel in an open spiral, take the needle underneath the next spoke ready to be worked.
3. Form a loop of thread over the surface of the spoke to be worked.
4. Take the needle down behind the loop of thread, bringing it up around the spoke and up through the loop of thread.
5. Pull to form a knot.
6. Keep working the wheel until the desired size has been achieved, stopping at spoke A.
7. Finish by winding the thread out along spoke A.

Hints and tips

Always try to maintain a good tension on the wheel, as it can easily become limp. When pulling the knot, make sure that the thread from the previous knot is taut so that there is something secure to pull against. The actual knot may have to be tugged right and left slightly to tighten it firmly. Use a thread or yarn that will stay held as a knot and will not become too loose.

Creative drawn thread work samples

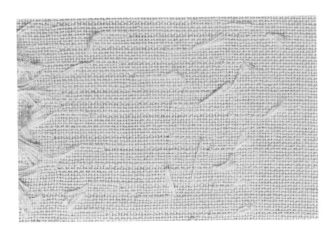

Drawn lines

This very light and delicate sample is worked with the ground fabric only. The horizontal threads are withdrawn, cut from the middle and rewoven back into the ground fabric, leaving the ends uncut on the surface. Every third or fifth thread horizontally has been withdrawn, the lines alternating at the ends, with some threads being withdrawn further back than others.

Drawn blocks

This half-worked sample shows random blocks of horizontal withdrawn threads. Threads are cut in blocks of up to ten threads of the fabric. The threads are withdrawn from the weave, but left on the surface unwoven. Hemstitching is worked randomly along the withdrawn blocks and beyond into areas not withdrawn. The ends of the working threads are not secured, but left on the surface with the withdrawn threads. A self-coloured thread and a variegated cotton thread are used.

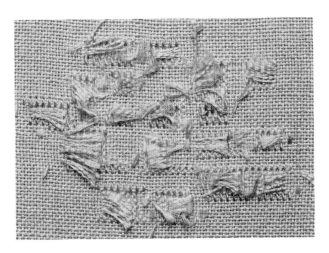

Drawn and unfinished blocks

Small blocks of withdrawn threads are worked within this sample. The individual blocks have anything between four and ten threads withdrawn and left unwoven on the surface. Both sides of each block are hemstitched with a thread withdrawn from the actual fabric.

Double, puckered and frayed

This sample is worked with two layers of evenweave fabric together, the same number of threads being removed from both the top and ground fabric for each border. The top fabric is applied onto the ground fabric and is pulled up in between each border, giving the whole sample a three-dimensional effect. The two fabrics are held together with the hemstitching on both sides of each border to group the threads. On the upper edge, variegated cotton thread is used which is of the same thickness as the threads of the fabric. The border patterns are simple, interlaced and knotted, linking both fabrics.

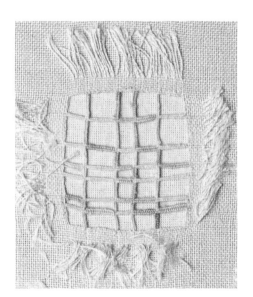

Heavily drawn

A large number of threads is withdrawn in this sample, leaving a skeleton two to three threads remaining in ratio to every eight to twelve withdrawn. The withdrawn threads are then rewoven back into the fabric over six threads and left on the surface uncut. The remaining bars are rewoven using self-coloured thread or a variegated cotton thread.

Parallel lines

Threads withdrawn in this sample are only removed vertically and then woven back into the fabric and left on the surface uncut. Between every eight to ten threads withdrawn, three to five are left. At each side of the sample, the threads are hemstitched, drawing them into pairs. The bars of threads that are not withdrawn are grouped on both sides at the same time, using herringbone stitch or a double-sided hemstitch, grouping the threads in pairs, but not necessarily the same two threads as on the neighbouring side.

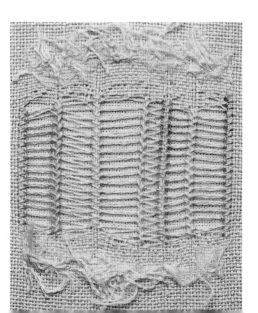

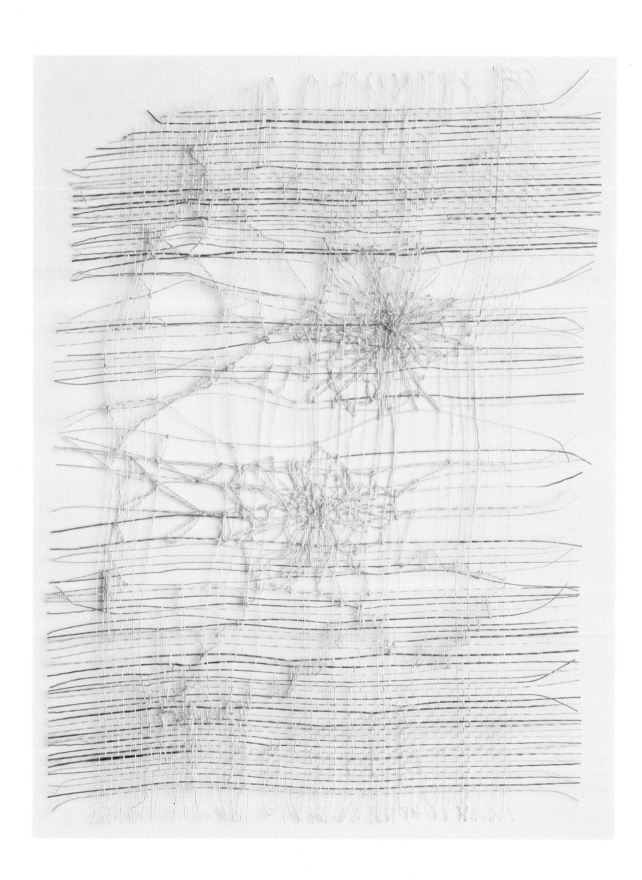

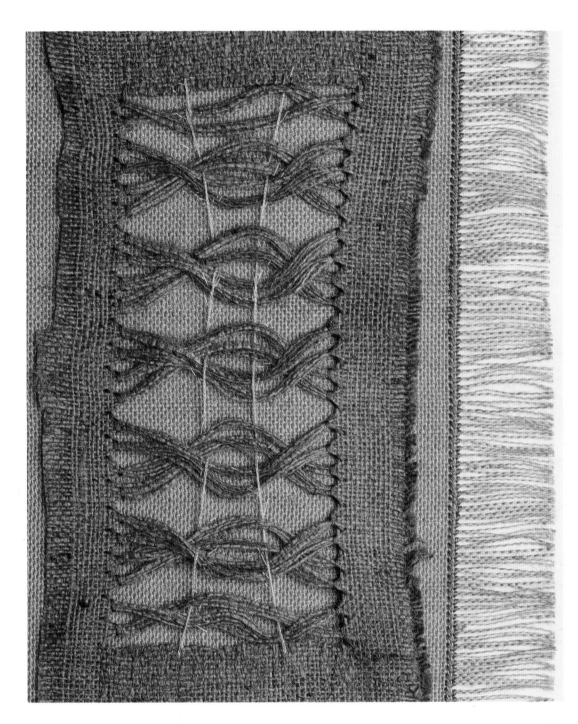

Left: *Blackberry Flowers*
Nicola Jarvis
Threads were removed from this coloured
evenweave grass fabric, and blackberry
flowers and leaves were worked into the
resulting framework.

Above: *Chunky hessian border*
Nicola Jarvis
The woven vertical threads of the fabric were cut and woven back to reveal the desired
space. The required numbers of horizontal threads were left and hemstitched into
bunches with stranded cotton. A simple interlaced border pattern was worked through
the middle of these bunches with a tea-dyed novelty thread called Frosty Rays.

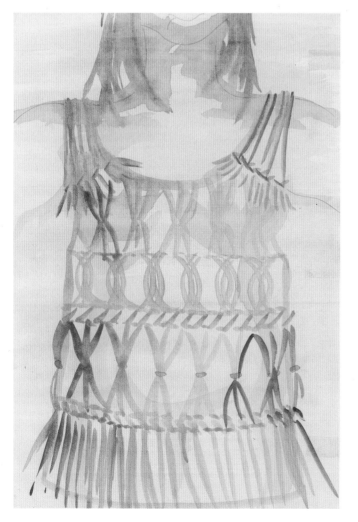

Above:

Fine hessian border

Nicola Jarvis

The horizontal threads of this fine-weight hessian were cut and drawn back to create a space in the fabric. The remaining vertical threads were hemstitched in Very Velvet novelty thread. A simple interlaced border pattern was worked in a thin nylon invisible thread along the centre of this pattern. Buttonhole stitch was also worked in the Very Velvet thread along the two shorter sides to complete the design.

Left:

Filigree tunic

Nicola Jarvis

Watercolour study proposing a design for a tunic worked entirely in a variety of large-scale drawn thread work border patterns. The shoulder straps are to be created by using withdrawn threads, and the edges are to be trimmed with fringing.

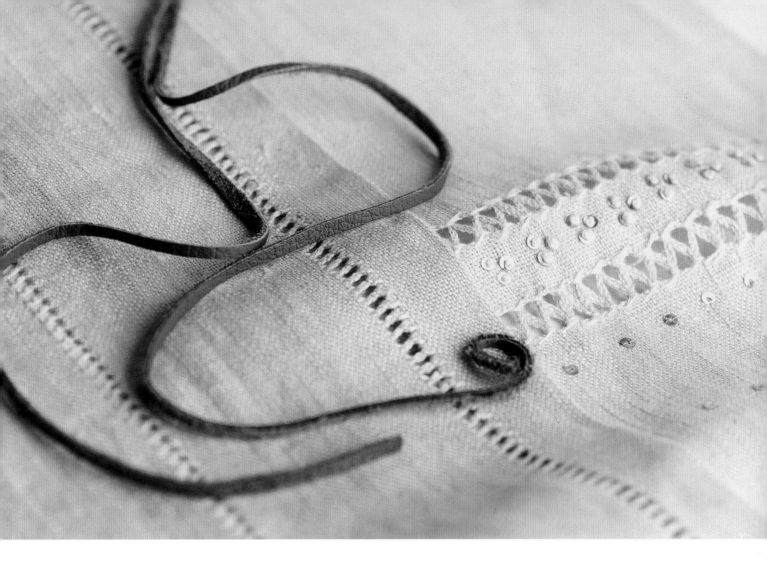

Above:
Skirt panel
Margaret Clementson
This skirt panel is worked on strong linen fabric, and has been patch indigo dyed. The drawn thread lines have been hemstitched and grouped or made into a fine detailed grid, with surface decoration worked with small sequins and French knots and a waistband woven with a soft leather thong.

Right:
Drawn thread panels
Margaret Clementson
All three panels are worked on silk crepe fabric. The weft threads are withdrawn and left in an unruly state or grouped with controlled hemstitching. The embroidery is detailed with solid French knots, glass beads, three-dimensional hand-woven flower heads and machine-embroidered lettering is cut and applied on top.

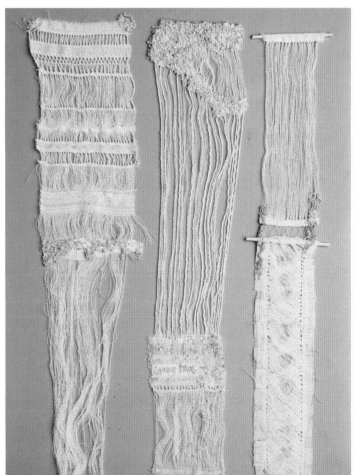

CHAPTER 6

Pulled work

18th-century Dresden work
With kind permission of the Royal School
of Needlework.

History

It has been suggested that pulled work was used to decorate garments worn by Cleopatra around 50 BC. Documentation also exists of pulled work executed in India dating back to AD 320–40. The stitch patterns were worked in silk thread on a fine, almost transparent, muslin ground.

Examples have been found of altar cloths from Germany decorated with pulled work that date from AD 1200. It can also be seen on various ancient textiles from Egypt, the Middle East and Peru. Coloured silks and metal threads were used to work the stitches.

From the 13th century, this technique developed in Europe and became particularly sophisticated, almost resembling needle-made lace. The availability and use of fine cambric and muslin in the 19th century caused pulled work to become very delicate. Some claim that pulled work was executed to imitate lace and it was for this reason that, like lace, it had a tax levied upon it. The intricate German derivative of this technique became known as Dresden work.

The base fabrics for pulled work have varied throughout history, depending on the region where each particular style evolved. In West Africa, it was worked on a raffia cloth. Stitch patterns in the Philippines were executed on a bark-cloth from the pineapple tree, in addition to hemp cloth.

Today, pulled work is still worked by hand on a range of evenweave fabrics. The choice of threads and fabrics is extensive because of the explosion in popularity of counted cross stitch.

Pulled work stitches

Horizontal chained border stitch

Horizontal chained border is also sometimes known as cable stitch.

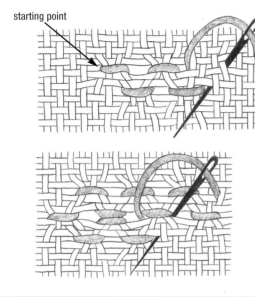

starting point

Method

1. Horizontal stitches are worked from right to left and from bottom to top alternately, working over *four* vertical threads each time, with *two* threads between both rows. Using a tapestry needle, work the first stitch, crossing over *four* vertical threads of the fabric.
2. Bring the needle up *two* threads of the fabric *above* and *back two vertical* threads.
3. Repeat the process, alternating bottom to top and top to bottom.
4. The second row is worked in exactly the same way, with the top row of stitches being worked into the bottom row of stitches already set.

Single faggot stitch

This stitch is worked diagonally from top right to bottom left. The diagonal stitch formation on the reverse side of the fabric causes the threads to become pulled together, therefore each stitch on the right side is a backstitch, worked in steps. Faggot stitch is worked over *three* threads in each direction as steps are formed.

Method

1. Using a tapestry needle, make a horizontal stitch to the reverse of the working direction.
2. Bring the needle up three threads down from the starting point, and again work backwards into a hole already formed by the previous stitch.
3. Repeat the process, bringing the needle up three threads in front horizontally, forming a diagonal stitch on the back, and again take the needle into the hole already formed.
4. Repeat the process, whether working downwards or upwards.

starting point

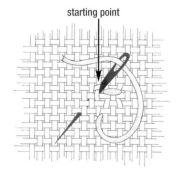
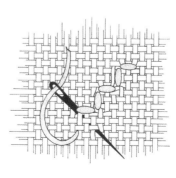

Honeycomb stitch

This stitch produces an attractive honeycomb effect.

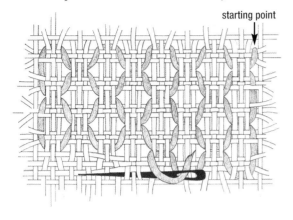

starting point

Method

1. Using a tapestry needle, make a vertical stitch over a count of *three* threads working *downwards*.
2. Now pass the needle under the evenweave fabric *three* threads along and *parallel*, and then work another stitch over *three* threads *upwards*.
3. Continue the pattern of stitches.
4. Work the next row in the same way, with the horizontal stitches at the back connecting and using the same holes.

Four-sided stitch

As the name suggests, this stitch is worked as a series of squares.

starting point

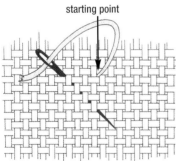

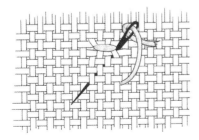

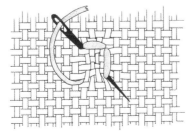

Method

1. Using a tapestry needle, work the first stitch from right to left *horizontally* over *four* threads.
2. Bring the needle out *diagonally* to the right, *four* threads below the starting point.
3. Take the needle down into the starting point and back up diagonally at the back towards the *bottom left* at a count of *four* threads.
4. Take the needle back up *vertically* to complete the third side of the square, bringing the needle up again at the *bottom right*, ready to begin the process again.
5. Work the next row in the same way, working the vertical stitches in connecting holes.

Hints and tips

Please note that the horizontal stitches sit at a slight angle, bottom left to top right. To keep the pattern consistent, make sure when working top to bottom or bottom to top that this remains so.

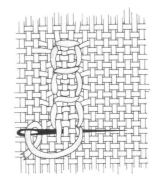
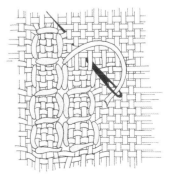

Diagonal raised band

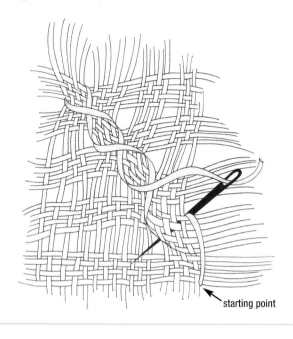

starting point

Method

1. Using a tapestry needle, work the first stitch vertically over *eight horizontal* threads of the fabric, as shown.
2. Bring the needle up again *diagonally* on the back, four vertical threads to the left and four horizontal threads downwards.
3. Repeat the process.
4. On the downward journey, the stitch is worked in the same way, using the same holes, with the stitch lying horizontally and crossing over the vertical stitches.
5. Pull the working thread tightly after each stitch is made.

Step stitch

Note that there should be no diagonal stitches on the back of this work, as a diagonal stitch would show on the front and the stitch would not be working the pulled work pattern correctly.

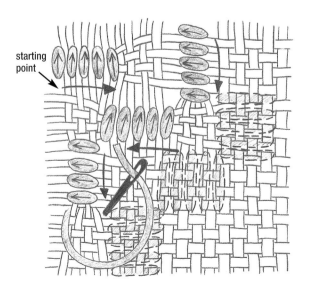

starting point

Method

1. Each diagonal row is worked in turn, either from bottom left to top right or top right to bottom left.
2. Work five stitches over four threads of the evenweave fabric each time.
3. Begin at the top right, by bringing the needle a count of four threads of the fabric below the top-right hole. Then take the needle into the top-right hole up over four threads vertically.
4. The block of stitches should be worked alternately vertically and horizontally.
5. Each block should link, sharing a hole with its neighbouring blocks in each corner.

Hints and tips

For simplicity, this may be worked one of two ways. If the vertical stitches are worked upwards over on the front, then the horizontal stitches should be worked from right to left on the front. Likewise, if the vertical stitches are worked downwards on the front, then the horizontal stitches should be worked from left to right on the front. Either way, they should be kept consistent.

Eyelets

Eyelets are made in a circular stitch pattern that involves forming a circle of stitches around one hole. They can be worked in a series or individually, and may be equal and uniform or random in shape. The circle can be any size and may be irregular in shape, and the stitches can be the same length or varying lengths, depending on the required effect.

Method

Stitches are formed using a tapestry needle, which should always come up at the edge of the eyelet, and down into the middle, making the middle the central pulling point.

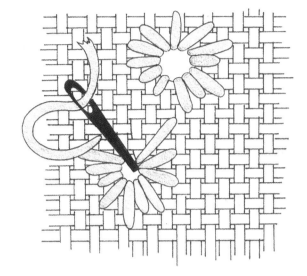

Ringed backstitch

Work ringed backstitch from right to left.

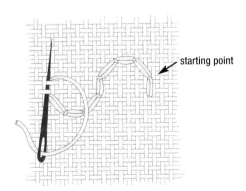

starting point

Method

1. Using a tapestry needle, work *two vertical backstitches*, over *two horizontal threads* of the fabric, using the same holes.
2. Bring the needle up again *two threads* both *horizontally and vertically* in front.
3. Work two backstitches back into the starting point, creating a diagonal on the front.
4. Work the next two horizontal straight stitches over two vertical threads of the fabric in the same holes.
5. Continue to work a series of alternating diagonal and straight stitches, creating the top half of the first ring and the bottom half of the next ring.
6. To finish, complete the last circle, and then complete each circle, working from left to right, pulling each stitch each time.

Creative pulled work samples

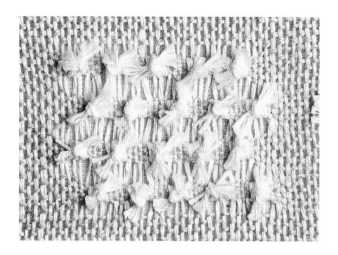

Pulled and knotted

This sample is worked with soft cotton and crochet cotton in one needle. A satin stitch block is worked over six threads of the fabric, with the ends of the thread left hanging at the start and finish of each block. These threads are finally pulled together into a knot, thus pulling the threads of the fabric. Each block is spaced apart by the same number of un-worked threads and each line alternates with the previous one.

Pulled fringed ends

This sample is worked using a linen thread looped around the horizontal threads of the fabric. Using a long length of thread, take the needle into the fabric, and then vertically back up six threads above. Take the needle back into the same hole, leaving a loop, and again back up the original hole. Thread both ends through the loop and pull. Trim the ends of the threads to the desired length.

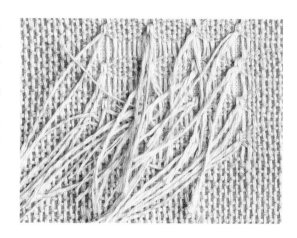

Randomly pulled

This sample is worked with a range of straight stitches, using a combination of fine soft cotton threads, one of which has a variegated colour. Apart from the stitches being straight, there is no discipline to this sample: the stitches are worked in random blocks, with the ends of the threads unfinished and lying on the surface of the work when the thread runs out. Each block is worked into the holes of the previous block, thus pulling the ground fabric.

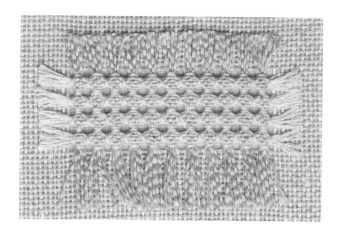

Doubled four-sided stitch

Two layers of fabric with the same count are used in this sample: one small piece on top of the ground piece. Line up the holes and threads of the fabrics and simply work four-sided stitch with a self-coloured thread through two layers, being careful that the same hole is hit each time on both layers. Once the stitching is finished, fray the top fabric to the edge of the stitching.

Diagonal chained border stitch, doubled and slashed

Two layers of fabric of the same count are laid together, with the holes and threads of the fabric in alignment. Diagonal chained border stitch is worked over the top with a variegated coloured cotton thread, working into the same holes at the top and bottom. Once the stitching is complete, the top fabric is carefully cut diagonally in between every three sets of stitches and then frayed back. This time the fabric will fray more because it is not cut along the grain, resulting in a more textured effect.

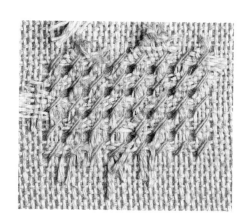

Blocked, doubled, cut and frayed

Again, two layers of the same count of fabric are laid together, with the holes and threads of the fabric in alignment. Work uniform blocks of satin stitch with self-coloured thread over three threads of the ground fabric, working five stitches with two blocks, worked above and below one another. Each set of two blocks is ten threads of the fabric apart, with six threads between rows. Once the stitching has finished, cut the top fabric in between the rows and each double block along the grain. Fray the top fabric up to the stitching around each satin stitch block.

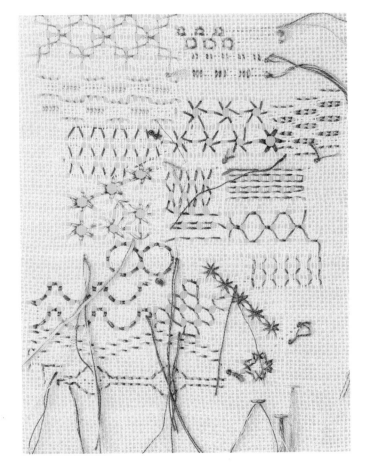

Left: *Frozen Leaves*

Eva Lotta Hansson

The source of this design came from looking at leaves frozen in puddles of water. The repeat patterns that emerged from this were so similar to that of pulled work that the transformation from an idea to the working model was a simple one.

The sample shows the test stitching for ideas that will be comparative to that of the design along with chosen colours to represent the colours within the photograph.

The picture on page 64 shows the actual piece of work as it was being embroidered, with the basting guidelines still in place. A mixture of thread colours and types may be seen and some surface stitching shows the stem of the leaf.

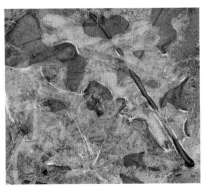

Left: *Pulled and Puckered*

Tracy A Franklin

The idea was to create pulled work with texture and to work on more than one layer of the same fabric. Only three stitches were used in this piece – four-sided stitch, three-sided stitch and a simple backstitch – worked with a mixture of natural coloured and hand-dyed threads of fine crochet cotton. Part of the top fabric was worked first of all before being applied to the base. The whole piece was an experimental exercise to see what could be achieved by working on one layer and working through two layers of fabric of the same count and by working up to the raw edges, allowing them to fray.

Bellis Perennis
Nicola Jarvis

The desire was to create a highly decorated surface on which to place a three-dimensional floral form with a white flower, chosen to symbolize femininity.

A common species was used to subvert the idea of preciousness and delicacy that can be associated with white embroidery, the daisy or *bellis perennis* being a small white hardy perennial that survives in many habitats.

Traditional rough household materials were incorporated into this piece – scrim, string, hessian, bleach, tea and wood – to allude to the domestic chores that have been performed by women throughout history.

A background pattern was designed to create the stylized floral effect around the raised daisy. It is worked on a base fabric of scrim. Immediately surrounding the focal flower is an area worked in four-sided stitch with silk floss and this has been edged with bone beads. Diagonal chained border stitch in tea-dyed string fills the next halo and bleached wooden beads form the outline. The outermost area is worked with hessian thread in honeycomb stitch.

Hessian fabric has been used for the three-dimensional daisy. Fine string outlines the edge of the petals in a random backstitch. The centre of the flower is stitched with ripped chiffon ribbons and loops of hessian thread. A large vintage button attaches the daisy to its background.

This piece was provisionally named 'Crazy Daisy' but I prefer the Latin name for daisy – *Bellis perennis*. Roughly translated, this means 'beautiful every/all years'.

CHAPTER 7

Shadow work

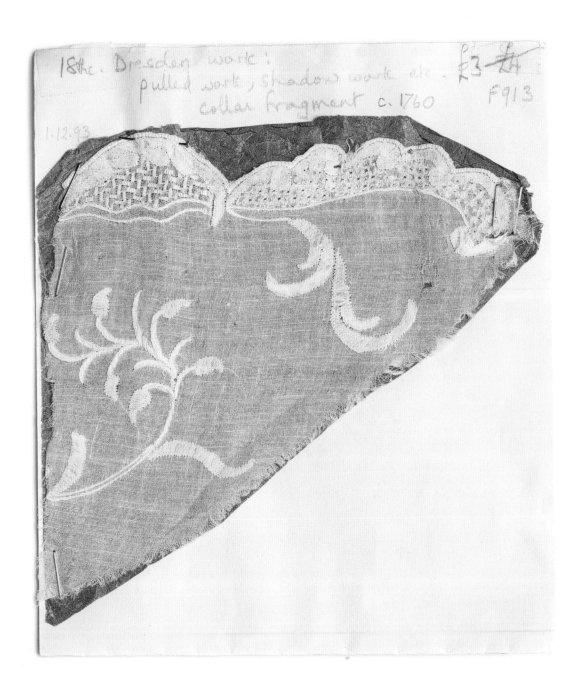

Collar fragment

This sample of 18th-century Dresden
work includes shadow herringbone stitch
and pulled work.

History

The ancient textile art of shadow work is thought to have originated in India, where it still enjoys popularity and is known as *chikankari*. The word *chikan* means 'embroidery'.

Traditionally worked in white threads on a sheer white ground, chikankari has its centre of excellence in Lucknow. This is a city situated in the Uttar Pradesh region in the north of India. Legend has it that Nur Jahan, the wife of the Mughal emperor Jahangir, introduced chikankari into this area.

The technique spread to a number of cities along the flood plain of the River Ganges, including Agra, Delhi and Rampur. Nevertheless, Lucknow is recognized as the main centre for this embroidery style.

Shadow work, which is a variation of chikankari work, is less ornate in appearance and is a technique that came to be worked on the reverse side of sheer fabrics. Herringbone stitch was worked within the design areas on the reverse side. This produced shadowy shapes apparently outlined in backstitch (actually the reverse side of the herringbone) on the front of the fabric. This is referred to as a 'reverse herringbone stitch' or 'closed herringbone stitch'.

Another type of shadow effect was created by cutting shapes from the same transparent fabric and applying them on the reverse of the sheer ground with an intricate stitch. This type of work has become known as shadow appliqué.

The use of coloured threads and fabrics has developed from the earlier monochromatic designs. Innovative coloured shadow work and shadow appliqué, executed both by hand and machine, have become very popular in home furnishings and women's fashions today.

Shadow work stitches

Use a fine embroidery needle and fine thread to create the best effects in shadow work. Stitch lengths can vary, but if you are using fine thread and fabric then the stitches must be kept small and consistent. Take care to conceal starting and finishing threads so that they are not seen through the sheer fabric.

Closed herringbone stitch

This is worked on the back of a transparent fabric in order to create a shadow on the front. On the right side of the fabric, two rows of backstitching will show, with the cross stitch in the background behind the transparent fabric.

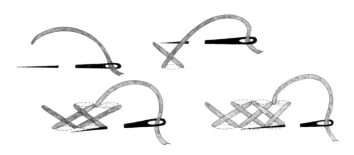

Method

Closed herringbone stitch is worked in exactly the same way as normal herringbone stitch (see page 93), except that the end of each stitch is worked into the hole of the next. The stitch follows the outline of the shape, and must start and finish right up to the furthest point of the motif, so that the outline looks complete on the front of the work. Work the stitch from left to right, with each individual stitch being worked from right to left, if right-handed, alternately along the two lines.

Hints and tips

Herringbone stitch can only span a certain width, depending on the design size and thread used. If the thread starts to loosen, then the area of the design needs to be halved and two rows of herringbone stitch should be worked side by side.

Be careful, when starting and finishing threads, to conceal the ends well so that they are not seen through the sheer fabric.

Trace the design on the wrong side of the fabric, but remember to mirror-image it before drawing, especially if the design includes any lettering.

Backstitch

Backstitch is used to create fine lines in shadow work. Unlike herringbone stitch, backstitch should be worked on the right side of the transparent fabric, as the long float stitches will appear on the back of the work.

starting point

Method

1. The stitch follows the outline of the shape of the design and can be worked from right to left, if you are right-handed. Start by bringing the needle up on the design line in front of the start point.
2. Take the needle back over into the starting point and back up in front of the stitch created. The lengths of stitches can be uniform in size or varied, depending on the effect required.

Hints and tips

A stem stitch will form on the wrong side of the fabric; try to keep the loop of thread on the same side of the needle each time, so that the backstitch appears more consistent on the front.

Pin stitch for shadow appliqué or quilting

Shadow appliqué or quilting offers an alternative to herringbone stitch, and is particularly useful for wider, larger areas.

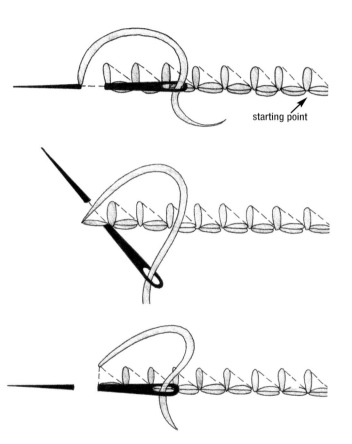

starting point

Method

1. It is worked using two layers of sheer fabric: the ground fabric and another piece, slightly larger than the desired finished motif or shape, which is applied to the back of the ground fabric with the grain lines matching. To prepare the two fabrics, tack (baste) them loosely together.
2. Work the pin stitch that is used to hold the two fabrics together from the front, stitching from right to left. Using an embroidery needle, begin by working a backstitch, followed by another backstitch directly on top, bringing the needle up diagonally opposite this time, as if working a square.
3. Now bring the needle out within the shadow quilting itself, and use this third stitch to hold the two fabrics securely together.
4. Once you have stitched around the whole shape, secure the thread and cut away the excess fabric from the back.

Hints and tips

Shadow appliqué or quilting can only be used up to a certain size, which depends on the design size and thread used. Larger areas need to be divided up into further sections.

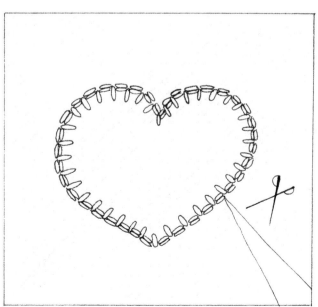

Creative shadow work samples

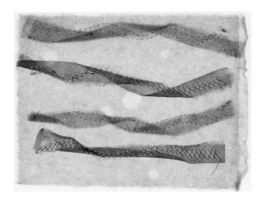

X-ray paper

This sample is worked on handmade layered paper. Strips of paper are applied to the front and back, the shapes being ripped or torn to produce edges that, when they are shadowed, may look either feathered or sharp. The strips of paper are bent and twisted, thus giving more layers, onto the main ground paper and are held by closed herringbone stitch, worked with one strand of white stranded cotton thread. The stitch, which is closed herringbone stitch, is twisted as it is worked over the paper so that, either from the back or the front, the full herringbone stitch contrasts with the two lines of backstitch when the piece is held up to the light.

Counted shadow blocks

This delicate sample is worked on organdie fabric, using one strand of white stranded cotton. The stitch is counted over the organdie, thus giving a very fine and controlled effect. Each horizontal stitch is taken over a count of two threads of the organdie, with the thread then trailing vertically on the back of the fabric over a count of between 10 and 20 threads, again with a horizontal stitch over the corresponding two threads on the opposite edge. The needle then comes back to the original line, trailing the thread behind again, and up at the end of the last stitch. Again a horizontal stitch is worked over a count of two threads and the process is repeated. Small blocks and longer blocks are worked, with the thread trailing more diagonally on the back, leaving spaces in between. Each line may be worked further to the left or further to the right in rows, which may be close together or spread apart, as desired.

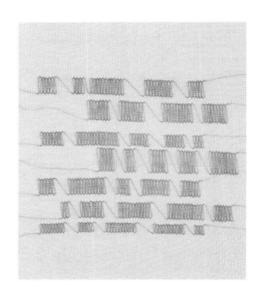

Layered circles

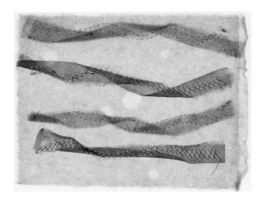

This sample is made with handmade petal paper circles, marked with a small coin. The circles of paper are cut out and placed on organza, both from behind and on top, giving a more laid effect. One by one, each circle is tacked (basted) around with a small running stitch, approximately 2mm (1/2in) from the edge of the paper. Note that the circles of paper are also overlapped, so that once the finished piece is held up to the light, more shadows are cast. The running stitch emphasizes each circle and adds extra detail to the transparent petals within the paper.

Circle waste

The handmade paper waste from the circles in the previous sample is used to produce this sample. The waste paper is placed as a mass on the back of the organza. Natural-coloured sewing thread is used to hold the paper in place in selected areas. Groups of three small stab stitches are used randomly to hold the paper together and against the organza, with the trail of thread from one group of stitches to the next being part of the whole effect. This sample, unlike the flat circles, is much more three-dimensional, with shadows being cast both up against the organza and lifted away.

Drawn shadow work

This sample is created purely from organza fabric. A strip of organza is ripped to give a light frayed edge. From this strip of organza, selected threads from the fabric itself are pulled up along the strip, and ruffled up to give a soft pleated effect, halving the length of the strip. The sample is then placed on the back of another piece of organza, which is taut and flat, and is held in position very casually, to hold the sample together while allowing it to have free expression. This sample is held using a small block of tiny stitches, worked with natural-coloured sewing thread.

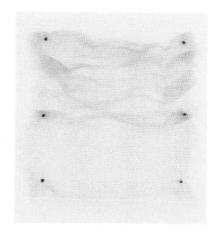

Puffball shadow work

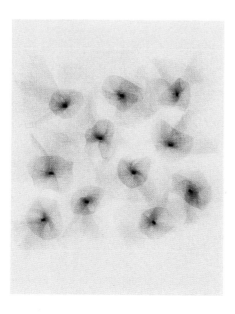

Again the effect of organza on organza is used to create this delicate and frivolous piece. Circles, approximately 5cm (2in) in diameter, are cut from organza. Each circle in turn is then gathered up by a small running stitch, worked with natural-coloured sewing thread, in a circle 2.5cm (1in) in diameter at the centre of the fabric. Keeping the same thread intact, the circle is pulled up, creating a bubble of organza. The thread is then wrapped two or three times around the organza at the neck of the running stitches, and then the needle and thread secures it further. Using the needle and thread, the gathered circle of organza is flattened out so that the organza looks like a circle on a circle. The needle is then brought up from behind and through to the front right, in the middle of the circle. Each circle of organza is then placed behind a taut piece of organza, to be held in place with a group of tiny satin stitches. This sample gives many depths of shadows, from the surface stitching to the bubble of organza and to the frayed edges of the circles right at the back of the work.

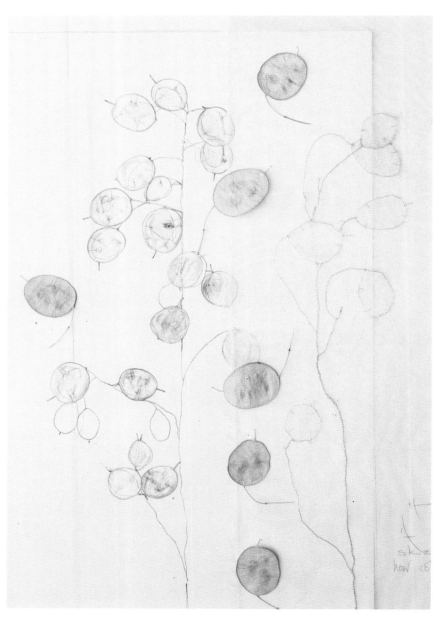

Left: *Honesty*
Margaret Clementson
Honesty or *Lunaria* is a biennial plant that
produces purple or white flowers. The seedpods
are large, circular and flattened, with large
seeds. A flat, thin-walled, translucent silicula is
formed during the ripening process, leaving the
'silver pennies' that are used in floral
arrangements.

The panel is worked on organza fabric,
doubled for the seed heads, and sewn by hand
over a core of threads to create the stiffly hairy
stem. The detail on the seed heads, also sewn
by hand, shows the delicacy and translucency of
the silver pod.

Right: *Decoration of the Skin*
Rachel Clowes
Skin decoration was used as a basis for this
work: the dress was produced to explore how
tattooed women are perceived, by using pattern
to reveal or conceal marks on the body.
Respectable clothing or a work uniform creates
a public image that may not reflect the true
personality of the individual. People who choose
to permanently embroider their skin with tattoos
display signs of identity, love and memories that
hold far more meaning than a removable pattern
or logo on clothing.

Intricate hand and machine embroidery was
used to create tattoos which pierce the fabric,
just as real tattoos are etched into the skin with
a needle. Clothing decoration has been
appliquéd over the top to create a delicate,
ghostly dress. Combining tattoos and pattern
from clothing creates a form of decoration
that is hard to define as belonging to either
the body or garment.

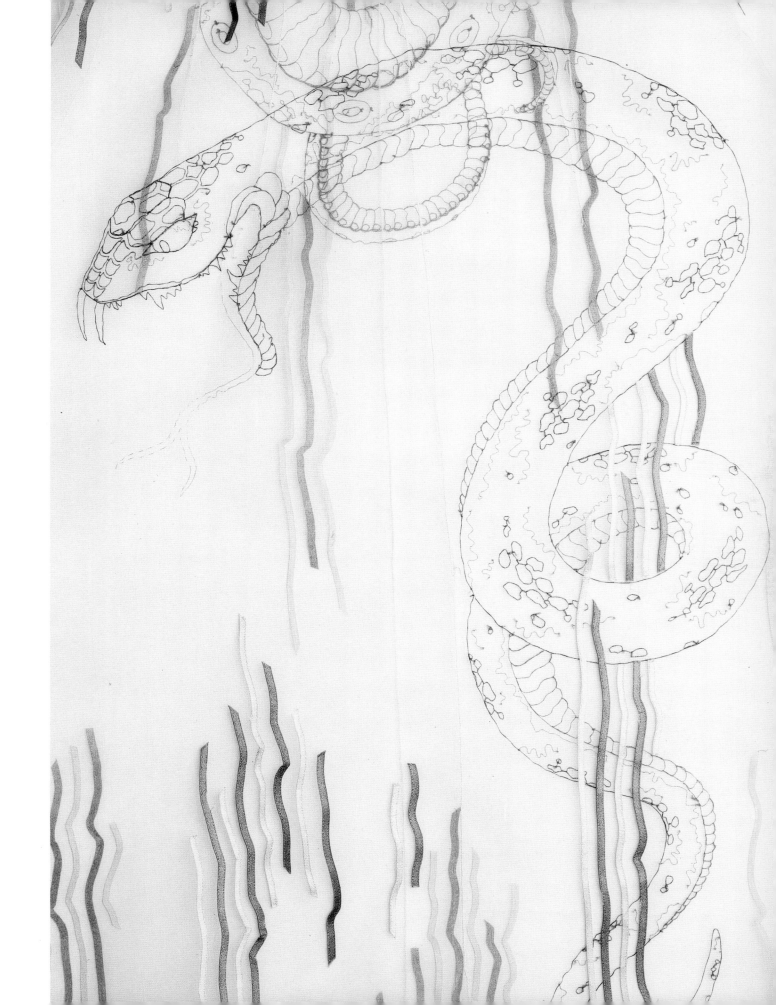

Architecture

Milagros Martin

This piece is worked in three layers, showing the carved pattern of
stone vaults and giving the feeling of depth by using surface work that
includes satin stitch and trailing on organdie to create the levels of
shadow. The top layer is worked in natural white, with the second layer
in creamier tones and the bottom layer in a more darkened tea colour,
to give the impression of looking into an empty, shadowy darkness.

Lampshade

Lyn Randall

I am fascinated by the surface quality produced as old wallpapers are torn away to reveal historical layers beneath. In each of these instances, a unique textural and visual story is displayed and I wanted to reflect this singularity by using techniques that would reproduce the layering, yet create a very unique and individual result. This small shade is created from a fine plastic. I emboss different textures into the plastic with papers and fabrics, both traditional and contemporary. I then layer these together with stitch to create a congruent yet completely unique surface that reveals its 'historical' layers when the light is turned on.

   Much of my inspiration comes from historical and contemporary wallpapers. I look at these not only in various museums, such as the V&A and the Geffrye in London, but also *in situ* as residential buildings are destroyed, as this is where you really get to see the layering effect. This is almost like the age rings of a tree, each layer recording a passing of time.

CHAPTER 8

Mountmellick and textural surfaces

History

Mountmellick work is a distinctive type of whitework embroidery. It derives its name from the town of Mountmellick, Co. Laois, Ireland, where it evolved and developed in the early part of the 19th century.

This white-on-white technique is worked in soft matt cotton thread on a closely woven fabric, known as 'satin jean'. It is a distinctive style of embroidery, with subtle richness and great elegance, producing the maximum effect with the minimum of stitches. It is exceedingly rich and effective in appearance and quite easy to execute once the mechanics of the stitches are learned.

Mountmellick was 'invented' by a lady named Mrs Johanna Carter and it was traditionally believed that she was a member of the Society of Friends (Quakers). An educational report of 1824, however, describes her as a member of the Church of Ireland. Mrs Carter was a designer and a manufacturer and ran a small school in the town, which was attended by as few as fifteen students, eight of whom were members of the Church of Ireland and seven of whom were Catholics.

Mountmellick was a boom town in the early 19th century, with a population of 8,000 and as many as 27 industries, including weaving, cotton spinning and milling. It was known as the 'Manchester of Ireland'. Fabrics were readily available and of reasonable cost, so Johanna chose to use cotton upon cotton, all in white.

The designs were based on nature, the favourite subjects being those that nature intended to be rough and knobbly in character, such as the bramble, dog rose, thistle, wheat and barley. The main criterion of Mountmellick design is that the motifs should pertain to the hedgerows of the Irish countryside.

Many of the stitches employed were the same as those used in crewel embroidery at the time, while numerous knotted stitches owe their origins to Johanna Carter and her students. These include the highly ornamental cable plait, which is extensively used to create bold stems and to outline leaves and flowers, creating a three-dimensional effect.

Mountmellick work is easily recognized by its distinctive characteristics:

- It is always white-on-white, embroidered with matt cotton thread upon satin jean fabric.
- There is an absence of eyelet holes or openwork.
- It features bold, natural floral designs, large in scale.
- The raised knotted stitches contrast with the smooth padded satin stitch, which is also a common feature.
- Almost all Mountmellick work is finished with a row of buttonhole stitches around the outside edge and is then completed with a knitted fringe. Occasionally, smaller items are finished with a pretty looped buttonhole fringe.

Mountmellick embroidery is extremely popular, not only in Ireland but throughout the rest of the world. Most needle artists find it both absorbing and fascinating.

Traditional Mountmellick embroidery
Loaned by kind permission of Marée D. Maher.

Mountmellick stitches

Depending on the fabric and thread size used, the size or length of stitches or the size of knots can vary.

Cable stitch
Although this stitch is worked on one design line, note that there is an upper and lower side to it.

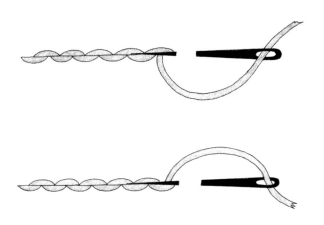

Method
1. Work this stitch along a design line from left to right. Start by bringing the needle up on the left and hold a loop of thread downwards on the surface of the fabric.
2. Take the needle down the width of the stitch desired on the design line and up again halfway back on the design line.
3. Pull up the stitch.
4. Work the same stitch again, this time holding the loop at the top, and bringing the needle back halfway to meet the first stitch, still working on the design line.
5. Continue to work in this way, alternating the loops at the top and bottom so that what looks like two rows of backstitch appear, alternating with each other.

Hints and tips
This stitch can be worked singly or in rows to create an overall texture.

Stem stitch
This stitch creates a rope-like effect.

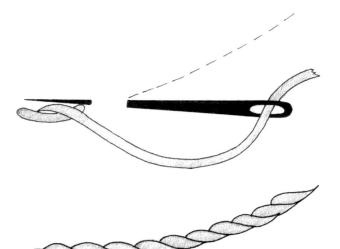

Method
1. Work this stitch along a design line from left to right. Start by bringing the needle up on the left and hold a loop of thread downwards on the surface of the fabric.
2. Take the needle down the width of the stitch desired on the design line and up again on the design line back halfway.
3. Pull up the stitch.
4. Repeat the same stitch, holding the loop downwards again and coming back up halfway along to meet the first stitch, still working on the design line.

Hints and tips
This stitch can be worked singly or in rows to create an overall texture.

Herringbone stitch

Herringbone is worked from left to right along an imaginary double line, with each stitch being worked from right to left, if you are right-handed, alternately along the two lines.

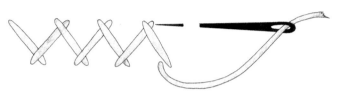

Method

1. Starting at the top left, work a stitch diagonally across towards the bottom right.
2. Bring the needle up on the lower imaginary line backwards, then across towards the top right, again taking a backstitch along the upper imaginary line.
3. Repeat, so that the herringbone cross stitch forms on the front of the fabric, with two rows of running stitches forming on the back of the work.

Hints and tips

This stitch can be worked singly or double, another herringbone stitch being worked over the top within the spaces left by the previous row.

Coral stitch

Coral stitch is worked from right to left along the design line.

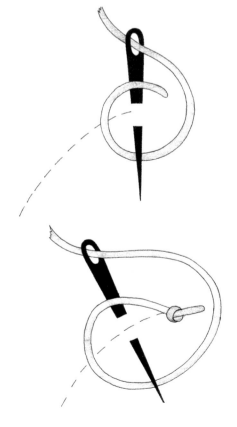

Method

1. Bring the needle up and begin by making a loop on the surface of the fabric.
2. Take the needle down just behind the loop, slightly above the design line, and up again within the loop just below the design line.
3. Pull the loop closed before pulling the needle through to ensure a tight knot, and then pull the needle through.
4. Continue the stitch.

Hints and tips

The knots can also be worked close together or spread apart but should be spaced evenly.

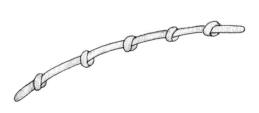

Chain stitch

This is worked from right to left along the design line or from top to bottom.

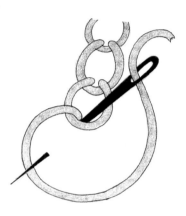

Method

1. Begin by bringing the needle up at the start of the line and back down the same hole, leaving a small loop on the surface of the fabric.
2. Bring the needle up further along the line, and up through the loop.
3. Pull up the loop, pulling away from it so that it does not close up too much.
4. Repeat the process, again taking the needle back into the same hole, which this time is inside the loop just made.
5. Again, create a loop and bring the needle up further along the line, and up through the new loop formed.

Hints and tips

Rows of chain stitch can be worked close together to create an overall effect and to cover a large area.

Couching

Two threads are used to create this couching stitch; one is laid flat along the design line and another working thread is used in the needle. The couching is worked from right to left along the design line.

Method

1. Begin by securing the laid thread at the right-hand side of the design line.
2. Also secure the working thread.
3. Bring the needle with the working thread up on the design line.
4. Pass the needle and thread over the laid thread at right angles into the same hole on the design line.
5. Continue working along the line in this manner.

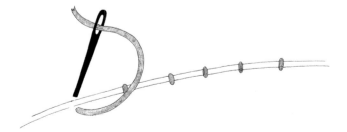

Hints and tips

Two different threads can be used, a thicker thread for laying and a finer thread for couching.

More than one thread can be couched at a time.

Stitches can be couched close together for dense coverage or far apart.

French knots

Remember that, depending on the thread type used, the knot size can vary.

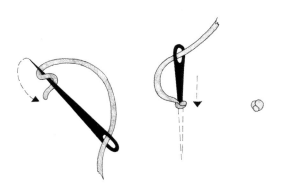

Method

1. Bring the thread up where the knot is to be positioned.
2. Hold the needle just above and parallel with the fabric, above the knot position.
3. Wrap the thread once around the point of the needle, as shown.
4. Holding the thread around the needle, move the point of the needle very close to where the thread came up (nearly the same hole but not quite).
5. Still holding the thread wrapped around the needle with one hand, use the other hand to pull the thread through to the back.
6. Gently pull the last loop of thread through to the back of the work, leaving a knot on the surface.

Bullion knots

A bullion knot differs from a French knot in having more wraps around the core thread. These knots are very three-dimensional, and can be worked in rows, as stem stitch or as individual stitches.

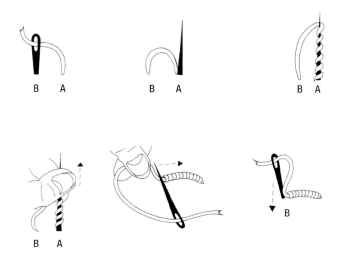

Method

1. Start by bringing the needle up through the fabric at point A.
2. Depending on the required size of the bullion knot, take the needle back into the fabric at point B, leaving a loop of thread on the surface.
3. Again bring the needle up at point A, the same hole, keeping hold of the needle underneath the fabric with one hand.
4. With the other hand, wrap the thread around the needle coming from hole A until it measures the distance between points A and B. (Measuring the distance can be done by tipping the needle over to point B.)
5. Once sufficient wraps have been made around the needle, use the hand on the surface to hold them in place, while bringing the hand from underneath to pull the needle through.
6. Keep the wraps flexible enough to allow the needle to pull through; if they are too tight, this will cause problems.
7. Once the needle and thread are pulled almost through, begin to tighten up the bullion knot by rolling it in between finger and thumb.
8. At this stage, it is easier to make the bullion knot tighter – once the thread is pulled right through to the surface, it is too late.
9. Pull the bullion knot the rest of the way to the surface of the fabric, using the needle to ease it that much further.
10. Take the needle right down at point B to finish.

Cretan stitch

A very versatile stitch, this can be used to fill broad or narrow shapes. It can be worked using either one or two central lines.

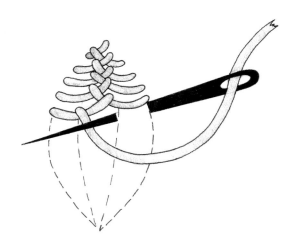

Method

1. Beginning near the top of the shape, bring the needle up on the left central line.
2. Take the needle down on the design line of the shape, on the left-hand side, angling the stitch downwards towards the centre line.
3. Leave the thread loose on the surface, forming a small loop.
4. Bring the needle back up again on the left central line, underneath the point where the needle came up previously, and pull *over* the loop of thread.
5. Repeat the process on the other side of the shape, taking the needle down on the design line of the shape and back up on the right central line within the loop of thread.
6. Continue to alternate from side to side, taking the needle down on the design line and up again within a loop of thread on the central line nearest to it.

Hints and tips

Always leave equal spacing between each stitch to give an overall even effect. The only exception is the very tip of the stitch, which may need to be more angled to fit within the shape.

The stitch can be worked either horizontally or at an angle, depending on where the needle is placed.

Stitches can be worked either close together or spread slightly apart, revealing the ground fabric.

Feather stitch

This stitch is worked in a similar way to chain stitch.

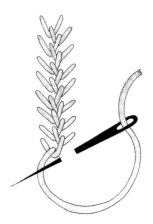

Method

1. Bring the needle up and form a loop.
2. Take the needle back down into the fabric, slightly lower and slightly across from the point where it came up.
3. Bring the needle back up again within the loop and repeat the process, this time taking the needle down on the opposite side, forming a loop in which to bring the thread back up through.
4. Repeat, alternating the thread from side to side.

Hints and tips

Stitches can be worked close together or spread apart depending on the effect required.

Fishbone stitch

This very versatile stitch can be used to fill broad or narrow shapes. The stitch is worked along two central lines in the same way as Cretan stitch.

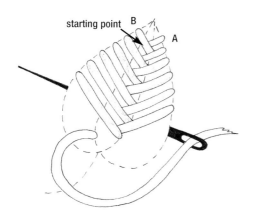

Method

1. Beginning near the tip of the shape, bring the needle up on the left central line and then back down again on the right design line.
2. Alternately form stitches on each side by bringing the needle up on one of the central lines and always taking it down on the opposite design line: for example, left central to right design line, then right central to left design line.

Hints and tips

Always leave equal spacing between each stitch to give an overall even effect. The only exception is the very tip of the stitch, which may need to be more angled in order to fit within the shape.

The stitch can be worked either horizontally or at an angle, depending on where the needle is placed.

Stitches can be worked either close together or spread slightly apart, revealing the ground fabric.

Fly stitch

Fly stitch is an open detached chain stitch.

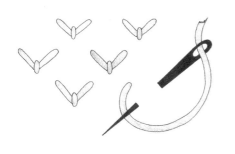

Method

1. The stitch forms a V-shape. Bring the needle up at the top left and back into the fabric at the top right.
2. Work the anchoring stitch, which forms the V and holds the thread below the level of the initial entry and exit points.

Hints and tips

This stitch can be worked in rows or as individual stitches.

The V can be long, wide or narrow depending on the effect required.

The holding stitch can be either small or long.

Trailing stitch

This is worked with two threads, one finer than the other. The thicker thread is laid as the core thread and the finer working thread is in the needle.

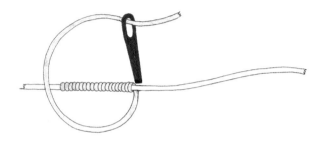

Method

1. Working along a design line, lay down your core thread.
2. Bring the working thread up on the line, over the core thread and back through the design line, very close to the point at which the needle came up.
3. Continue to couch over the thread, completely covering it.

Hints and tips

The core thread can be very fine or very thick depending on the effect required.

The core thread can be stranded, so that the trailing either grades from thick to thin or thin to thick.

Cable chain

It is important to keep a good tension on this stitch, as the loops can look too big and untidy.

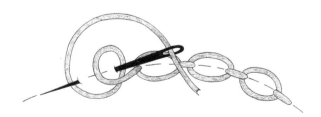

Method

1. Work this stitch along a design line, beginning by bringing the needle up with the working thread.
2. With the thread on the surface of the fabric, make a reversed loop by forming a loop and turning the loop upside down so that the thread coming out from the loop lies underneath the loop, thus forming another loop.
3. Take the needle into the first loop and come out in the second loop along the design line.
4. Adjust the loops so that they are not too big and repeat.

Hints and tips

The stitch can be worked with fine thread, with the stitches closer together to give a more lacy effect, or it can be worked with thicker thread and bigger stitches to give a bolder appearance.

Mountmellick stitch

When making the stitches, it may help to think of this stitch as an equal-sided square.

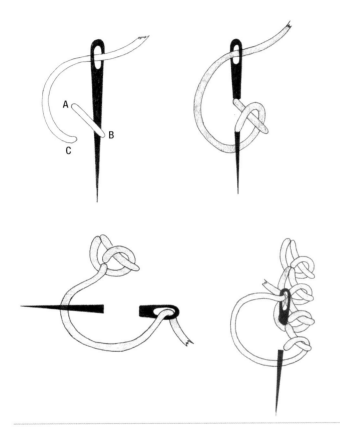

Method

1. Begin by bringing the needle up at A.
2. Take the needle down diagonally opposite at B and up at C.
3. Take the needle underneath the diagonal stitch formed without penetrating the ground fabric.
4. Form a loop on the surface of the fabric. Take the needle back through point A and up again at point C, through the loop of thread.
5. Continue the stitch in the same way.

Hints and tips

The stitch can be worked on a bigger or smaller scale as required, with either thicker or finer thread, as appropriate for your design.

Split stitch

The finished effect of this stitch resembles a fine chain stitch.

Method

1. Work along a design line, beginning with a small single stitch.
2. Bring the needle up right through the centre of the stitch.
3. Next, take the needle forward and back through the fabric on the design line, and then repeat.

Hints and tips

This stitch can be worked with bigger or smaller stitches, using fine or thicker thread.

Rows of this stitch can be worked close together to cover a large area.

This stitch can be used as a line of padding for long and short stitch or for satin stitch.

Satin stitch

This is worked over a split stitch outline, which helps to create a better shape for the satin stitch by slightly raising the outline.

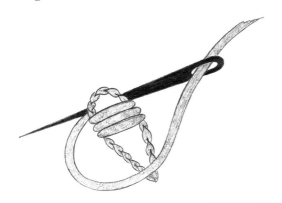

Method

1. First work split stitch around the shape.
2. Start in the middle to achieve good direction, bringing the needle up from behind the split stitch.
3. At right angles to the shape, take the needle back over the other side, angling the needle around the split stitch.
4. Continue to work from the middle out to one side and then from the middle out again to the other side, as shown in the diagram always bringing the needle up on the same side and keeping the stitches very close together.

Hints and tips

Always keep the stitches very close together and parallel with one another.

Seeding

This is a pattern formed of small stitches, all the same length, sewn in random directions on the ground fabric.

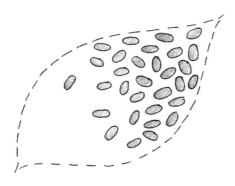

Method

When working seeding, keep the stitch length consistent, the direction of the stitch random, and look at the space around each stitch to ensure that they are evenly distributed.

Hints and tips

Seeding stitches can vary in length: you may either make very short stitches or longer ones. It is important, however, to keep the length consistent within an area and the spaces around them even.

Seeding stitches can be worked very close together and spread further out within a shape to create a fading effect.

Seeding can be worked in various different ways: as two parallel stitches together in an equals sign, or in a V-shape, or like a division sign and so on.

Long and short over split stitch

This stitch is the first stage in shading.

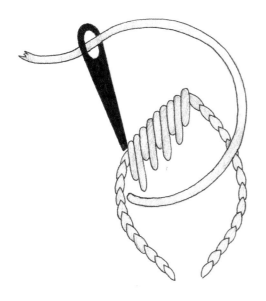

Method

1. Begin by split-stitching the shape.
2. Next, start in the middle by bringing the needle up within the shape and working *over* the split stitch, angling the stitches in slightly.
3. Continue to work from the middle out down one side of the shape, always coming up within the shape and down over the split stitch edge.
4. Keep the stitches close together, varying the lengths so that they appear alternately longer and shorter.
5. Once one side is worked, return back to the middle and work down the other side.

Hints and tips

Always keep the first row of long and short stitch a good length. This row will need to be shaded into, and if the long and short stitches are too short, then there will be no scope for shading. This will make the piece look very 'stitchy'.

When working down the side of a leaf, the side becomes very steep, and it may therefore be difficult to work long and short stitch, which means that the stitches become more or less the same length and are just 'stepped' instead.

Shading

Once the split stitch edge and the first stage of long and short have been worked, it is then possible to start shading.

Hints and tips

It is important to keep the stitch lengths long enough to allow shading: too small and the effect will appear very 'stitchy'; too long, however, will look stilted. Always consider the shape being shaded. The stitches should be placed randomly in the set direction. If lines emerge where the needle is brought up, then stitches are not random enough.

Method

1. Again, begin in the middle by bringing the needle up within the long and short stitches.
2. This time the shading is worked *down* and *over*, compared to the long and short stitch, which was worked up and over.
3. Following the direction made by the long and short row, take the needle down into the fabric.
4. Again, next to this first stitch, bring the needle up within the long and short row, but maybe higher up this time; the next stitch may then be a little lower. Bring the needle up randomly each time, as this will give a smoother effect and avoid a rigid line forming.
5. The stitch length is more or less the same each time – no longer long and short, just randomly placed for a natural look.
6. Eventually, the idea of rows of stitches should disappear as the stitches should just merge into one another, giving a smooth appearance when stitching is complete.

Creative textural samples

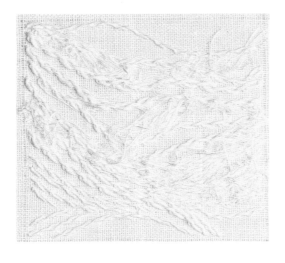

Cable chain on frayed silk
Cable chain stitch is worked in various thicknesses of numbers – 2, 3 and 4 – Mountmellick threads. The cable chains are worked in contour lines over natural-coloured fraying strips of silk fabric. Cable chain stitch is explained on page 98.

Pleated herringbone stitch
Using soft cotton thread, closed herringbone stitch is worked over pleated fraying strips of fine linen fabric. The stitches range from very wide to narrow in order to create an overall texture.

Raised interlocking herringbone stitch
Fabric rolls of soft cotton strips of fabric are laid on the surface on the ground fabric and then buttonholed over the top with no. 2 Mountmellick thread. Stitch one side of the fabric to hold the rolls of fabric down and then the other side as decoration, interlocking with the spokes of the first row of buttonhole stitch.

French knots with silk waste

Silk pod waste was used to create this individual three-dimensional texture, created with French knots. The silk pod was pulled and frayed to show it in its natural raw form when it is teased apart. French knots, worked with no. 4 Mountmellick thread, were used to hold it into position. These were set in groups and were also seeded apart to create an overall effect.

Paper contour lines

Natural handmade paper was torn into small pieces, dampened and manipulated by puckering the surface, and then left to dry. The paper was then placed onto the ground fabric and held down with running stitches worked with no. 3 Mountmellick thread in contour lines, allowing the paper to pucker and slightly fray out.

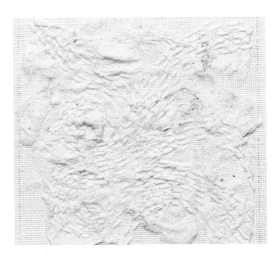

Embossed fishbone stitch

This fossil effect is worked in fishbone stitch on natural-coloured kitchen paper towel, which has been ripped apart and placed randomly on the ground fabric. The fishbone stitch has been worked with no. 3 Mountmellick thread into lines that may be straight or curved and run in random directions.

Grouped bullions

A mass of bullion knots has been worked in one concentrated area in loops, laying and clambering over one another to create a very three-dimensional, maggot-like effect. Worked in numbers 2, 3 and 4 Mountmellick thread, the bullion knots have more winds than there is space, thus making them stand away from the fabric itself, with each knot being pulled taut.

Couched lines and circles

Couching is worked in circles with soft cotton thread. One length is in the needle and is used to couch over laying threads of from one to six strands, laid in swirls and circles, and giving various contrasts in height and texture. As couching is worked, it is possible to start with one strand of soft cotton and gradually increase, or with six strands of soft cotton and gradually decrease.

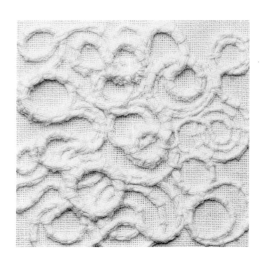

Chunky cable braids

Bands of cable plait stitch are worked in curved lines, overlapping and climbing over one another. No. 4 Mountmellick thread is used double to create a very 'chunky' effect. The stitch is basically worked in between two parallel lines, the needle being brought from the right-hand side to the left. As the needle is taken into the fabric on the right-hand side, a loop of thread is wrapped around it and then another loop is created on the left-hand side as the needle is brought up again. The stitch must be left loose as it easily pulls into itself.

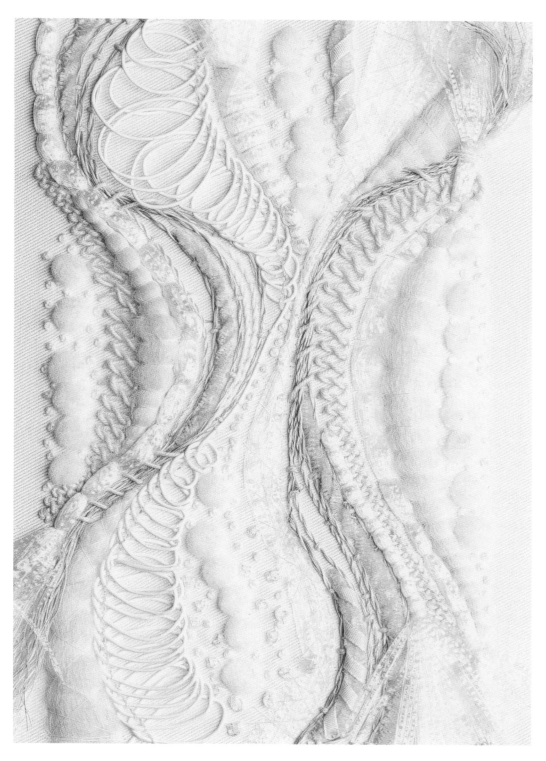

Onion
Emi Nimura
The panel combines
surface stitches, including
herringbone stitch and
French knots, with
couching.

Threads used:
• Mini pompom
• Cord for paper motif
  work
• Sashiko thread
• Ivory cotton thread
• Ribbon for ribbon
  embroidery
• Wool for weaving
• Knitting yarn
• Nylon string for packing
• Raffia

Above: *Blouse*

Surface stitching detail on a blouse using a bullion braid and French knots.

Right: *The Old Oak Bark*

Owen Davies

The brief was to work a piece of contemporary whitework embroidery inspired by the texture of Mountmellick work; any media can be used as long as it is embroidered and it must be white or natural tones, thus showing the texture.

The idea – on receiving the brief, first thoughts were 'white pure and virginal'. This led to thinking about Queen Elizabeth I – the Virgin Queen. Research into history of that period led to thinking of a design that would enable the technique to be worked while still creating a contemporary piece of work. Therefore the idea was to link the Elizabethan era to the present day.

The technique needed to be approached in a way that had not been seen before. With the Virgin Queen in mind, I made a trip to the residence where she first heard that Mary Tudor had died and she had become queen. Rich parklands surround Hatfield House where the old Palace of Hatfield stands. Here stood the oak tree where Elizabeth first heard the news that she was to be queen.

The aim was to create, in a contemporary style, a section of an Elizabethan oak tree, using known and unknown skills. The inspiration came from the idea of embroidering an old oak that stands in the Elizabethan parkland, a tree Elizabeth herself may have seen growing as a sapling. The oak in mind had been gnarled, furrowed and twisted. The texture and complex forms of the bark allowed experimenting with a great variety of threads and materials, ranging from basic packing string to the finest pure silk thread. The embroidery has been worked into waste silk cocoon pods, used to create the bark. Areas of the tree have been applied as a slip and paper has been applied and stitched into.

With thanks to Jacqui Carey of the Carey Company, who has made a variety of hand cords that have been applied onto the 'Old Oak Bark' and also to Nicola Kurtz for the bark photography.

CHAPTER 9

Ayrshire and fine whitework

History

Ayrshire whitework is named after a county in south-west Scotland and is sometimes referred to as 'Scottish flowering' or 'sewed muslin'. It was one of the few forms of whitework that developed on a commercial scale, flourishing from the 1820s to the 1860s.

Traditionally, this technique is executed on fine cotton muslin with fine cotton thread. Ornate floral and curvilinear motifs are worked in padded satin stitch, stem stitch and intricate filling patterns in cut areas.

This fine whitework technique adorned baby garments, especially christening robes and bonnets, and women's dresses, with elaborate detailing on the collars, cuffs, caps and petticoats. Men's shirt ruffles were also decorated in this way.

In early Ayrshire work, pulled and drawn fillings were used. This was until an entrepreneurial lady, Mrs. Jamieson, the wife of an Ayr cotton agent, saw a French christening robe with needlelace fillings. She taught these needlepoint and buttonhole techniques to the embroiderers, who gradually accepted them, working to a high standard.

The designs were professionally printed from wooden blocks up until 1837, with earlier motifs being quite large. After 1837 designs were lithographed.

The decline of the industry coincided with the interruption of the cotton trade caused by the American Civil War between 1861 and 1865, when the blockade cut off the supply of raw cotton from the southern states to Britain. Finally, when trade did recover, a change in fashions in the 1870s led to a decline in the demand for whitework, causing the industry to fade rapidly.

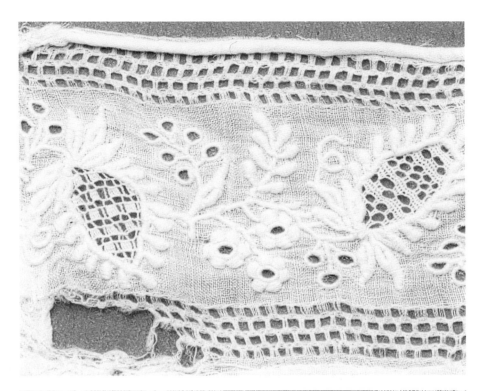

Sample of very fine Ayrshire whitework
with needlelace fillings, c. 1840.

Frill or border with very fine surface
whitework, c. 1830.

Ayrshire whitework stitches

Corded Brussels for open fillings

Fine or thicker threads can be used to work this filling stitch, which can be worked solid or open, depending on the effect required.

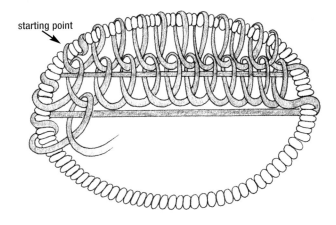

starting point

Method

1. Begin by securing the thread at the top left-hand side of the hole.
2. Start working the thread from left to right along the top edge of the hole by making a very loose buttonhole stitch. Take the needle down into the top edge of the hole, and come up through the loop of thread.
3. Once the thread has reached the right-hand side, secure it; take the thread back over to the left-hand side, just underneath the loops, and again secure it.
4. Again, work buttonhole stitch from left to right by taking the needle down through the loops made by the first row and catching the single thread thrown across.

Hints and tips

Try to keep the stitches evenly spread so that they do not become too crowded, making it difficult to embroider into them.

Keep each line straight. If you are working a rounded shape, the top and bottom rows will be shorter.

Double Brussels for open fillings

As with corded Brussels, fine or thicker threads can be used to work this filling stitch, which can be worked either solid or open, depending on the effect required.

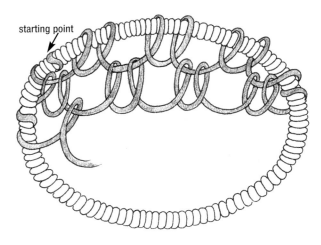

starting point

Method

1. Begin by securing the thread at the top left-hand side of the hole.
2. Start working the thread from left to right along the top of the hole by working a very loose buttonhole stitch. Take the needle down into the top edge of the hole, and come up through the loop of thread.
3. Once at the right-hand side, secure the thread and bring it up again, slightly lower, to begin the next row.
4. Buttonhole from right to left into the first row, working two stitches into one loop and then jumping two buttonhole stitches on the first row so that each row alternates with the previous one.

Hints and tips

As for corded Brussels stitch.

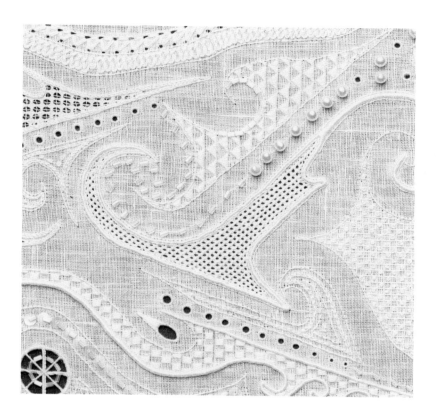

Abstract panel
Helen McCook
This piece is worked on fine linen fabric and incorporates all the elements of traditional fine whitework, including counted surface work, pulled work, small eyelets and cut eyelets with beads, heavy trailing and stem stitch.

Geneva Dandelions
Florence Collingwood
A small panel incorporating traditional techniques with a net lace ribbon insert. It includes satin stitch, trailing, eyelets and pulled work.

Floral Explosion

Lisa Bilby

A fine piece of whitework, based around the principles of Richelieu work, this was originally designed by sketch and developed. It is worked on linen cambric with a combination of organza, white metal purl, stranded cotton, lace threads (nos 30, 50 and 80), and coton à broder no. 16.

Both traditional and contemporary stitches and materials are used, including padded satin stitch, half ladder stitch, beading, raised areas with wired organza petals, round and oval eyelets, backstitch wheels, wrapped metal purl, stem stitch and chain stitch.

Collars and cuffs

Amanda Clayton

Amanda shows a contemporary approach to whitework techniques, using surface work, layering of fine fabrics, and some cutwork, while giving the whole piece a vintage look.

Fabrics and threads that have been used in Amanda's work include:
- Pina cloth – made from pineapple fibres and sometimes boil-washed to help with the vintage look
- Silk satin fabric
- Silk chiffon fabric
- Silk net
- Silk floss thread
- Rayon floss thread

CHAPTER 10

Further experimental work

Blossom

Clare Hanham

A simple embroidery worked on a fine cotton and embellished with stranded cotton incorporating iridescent thread. Before embarking on the design, the embroiderer pulled together many different images of blossom and then chose just one of them to produce the design.

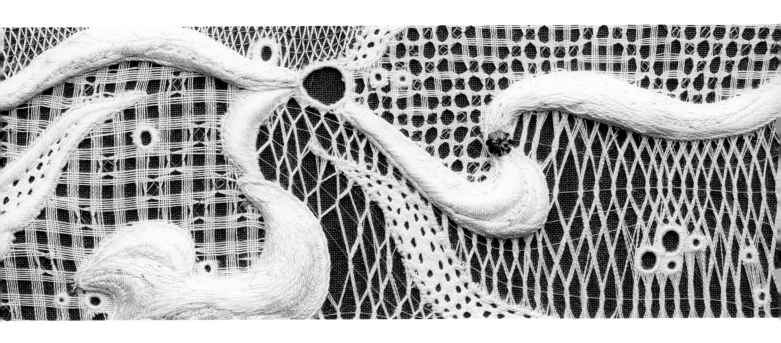

Japanese Wave
Jennifer Goodwin
The design inspiration was taken from the Japanese wave patterns of Hiroshige and was used to explore contrasts with textures, solid areas and open areas, freeness of design and rigidity of technique. The background has very open drawn thread work, with many threads removed from the ground fabric to contrast with the high raised solid areas, which were worked separately and applied on top. Metallic and fine threads were used for added interest, with a dark-coloured jewel to contrast with the dark background fabric.

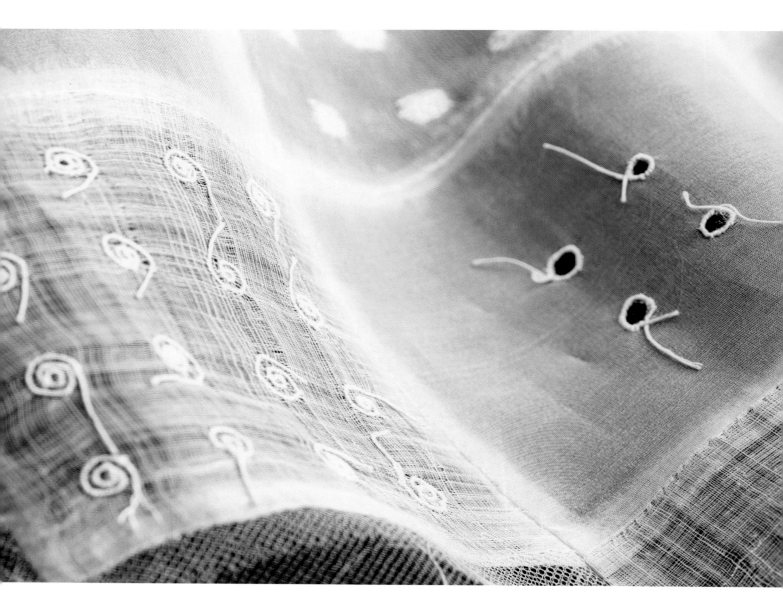

Vintage panel

Amanda Clayton

Panel showing different techniques created
using various fabrics including pina cloth, silk
chiffon and silk net, and threads including silk
floss and rayon.

Further reading

Brittain, Judy. *Good Housekeeping Step-by-step Encyclopaedia of Needlecraft*, Ebury Press

Bryson, Agnes F. *Ayrshire Needlework*, B T Batsford

Cave, Œnone. *Linen Cut-Work*, Vista Books

Dawson, Barbara. *Whitework Embroidery*, B T Batsford

de Dillmont, Thérèse. *Encyclopaedia of Needlework*, DMC Library, Mulhouse (France)

Digges, Mary-Dick, Fehd, Dolly Norton, Lawson, Nancy and Vogt, Martha Pearle. *Lady Evelyn's Needlework Collection*, Embroidery Research Press, Inc. Roswell, GA

Drysdale, Rosemary. *Pulled Work On Canvas and Linen*, Charles Scribner's Sons, New York; Bell & Hyman: London

Earnshaw, Pat. *The Identification of Lace*, Shire Publications

The Essential Guide to Embroidery, Murdoch Books

Houck, Carter, ed. *Whitework: Techniques and 188 Designs*, Dover

Houston-Almqvist, Jane. *Mountmellick Work: Irish White Embroidery*, Colin Smythe

Leach, Agnes M. *Drawn Fabric Embroidery*, Edward Hutton, London

Mary Thomas's Dictionary of Embroidery Stitches, Hodder & Stoughton

Mary Thomas's Embroidery Book, Hodder & Stoughton

McNeill, Moyra. *Drawn Thread Embroidery*, B T Batsford

McNeill, Moyra. *Pulled Thread Embroidery*, Dover Publications

Mountmellick Work: Irish White Embroidery, A Practical Workbook, Treacymar Publishing Co

Needlework School, The Embroiderers' Guild Practical Study Group, Windward

Prickett, Elizabeth. *Ruskin Lace and Linen Work*, B T Batsford

Snook, Barbara. *Embroidery Stitches*, Dryad Press

Swain, Margaret. *Ayrshire and Other Whitework*, Shire Publications Ltd

Swain, Margaret. *The Flowerers: the Story of Ayrshire White Needlework*, W & R Chambers

Wark, Edna. *Drawn Fabric Embroidery: A Guide to Pulled Thread Work*, B T Batsford

Warner, Pamela. *Embroidery, A History*, B T Batsford

Weldons Encylopædia of Needlework, The Waverley Book Co

Wilson, *Erica*. *Erica Wilson's Embroidery Book*, Faber & Faber

Suppliers and contacts

Thread and fabric stockists

Coats Crafts UK
P O Box 22
Lingfield House
Lingfield Point
McMullen Road
Darlington
County Durham DL1 1YQ
Tel: 01325 394237
www.coatscrafts.co.uk
Email: consumer.ccuk@coats.com

Copeland Linens Ltd
50 Boundary Street
Belfast BT13 2EJ
Tel: 02890 321065
Fax: 02890 322786
www.copelandlinens.com
Email:
copeland.linens@btclick.com

DMC Creative World Ltd
Pullman Road
Wigston
Leicestershire LE18 2DY
Tel: 0116 2811040
Fax: 0116 2813592
www.dmc.com
Email: dmc@dmccreative.co.uk

Empress Mills (1927) Ltd
The Empress Centre
Glen Mill
North Valley Road
Colne
Lancashire BB8 8SS
Tel: 01282 863181
Fax: 01282 870935
www.empressmills.co.uk
Email: chris@empressmills.com

Mace & Nairn
PO Box 5626
Northampton
NN7 2HE
Tel: 01604 864869
Fax: 01604 864924
www.maceandnairn.com
Email:
enquiries@maceandnairn.com

Madeira (UK) Ltd
12 Hallikeld Close
Barker Business Park
Melmerby
Ripon
North Yorkshire HG4 5GZ
Tel: 01765 640003
Fax: 01765 641707
www.madeira.co.uk
Email: info@madeira.co.uk

Macculloch & Wallis Ltd
25–26 Dering Street
London W1S 1AT
Tel: 020 7629 0311
Fax: 020 7629 8097
www.macculloch-wallis.co.uk
Email: macculloch@psilink.co.uk

Oliver Twists
22 Phoenix Road
Crowther
Washington
Tyne and Wear NE38 0AD
Tel: 0191 4166016
Fax: 0191 4153405
Email:
jean@olivertwists.freeserve.co.uk

Pearsalls Embroidery Silks
Tancred Street
Taunton
Somerset TA1 1RY
Tel: 01823 274700
Fax: 01823 336824
www.pearsallsembroidery.co.uk
Email:
sales@pearsallsembroidery.com

Sew-it-all Ltd UK
The Warehouse
24 Chandos Road
Buckingham
Buckinghamshire MK18 1AL
Fax: 01280 814 818
www.sewitall.co.uk
Email: info@sewitall.co.uk

Vari-galore Embroidery
5 Bennet Close
Alton
Hampshire GU34 2EL
Tel: 01420 80595
Fax: 01420 80595
www.varigalore.com
Email: lorna@varigalore.com

Fabric stockists

Borovick Fabrics Ltd
16 Berwick Street
London W1F 0HP
Tel: 020 7437 2180 / 0520
Fax: 020 7494 4646
www.borovickfabricsltd.co.uk
Email: borovickfabrics@btclick.com

The Silk Route
Cross Cottage
Cross Lane
Frimley Green
Surrey GU16 6LN
Tel: 01252 835781
www.thesilkroute.co.uk
Email: hilary@thesilkroute.co.uk

Whaleys (Bradford) Ltd
Harris Court
Great Horton
Bradford
West Yorkshire BD7 4EQ
Tel: 01274 576718
Fax: 01274 521309
www.whaleys-bradford.ltd.uk
Email: whaleys@btinternet.com

Willow Fabrics
95 Town Lane
Mobberley
Knutsford
Cheshire WA16 7HH
Tel: 0800 056 7811
Fax: 01565 872239
www.willowfabrics.com
Email: care@willowfabrics.com

Paper

Paperchase
213 Tottenham Court Road
London W1T 9PS
Tel: 020 7467 6200
www.paperchase.co.uk
Email: write@paperchase.co.uk

Antique embroideries

P & A Antiques Ltd
42 Havelock Road
London SW19 3HD
Tel: 020 8543 5075
Fax: 020 8404 6262
www.pa-antiques.co.uk

Classes, courses and further information

Embroiderers' Guild
Apartment 41
Hampton Court Palace
East Molesey
Surrey KT8 9AU
Tel: 020 8943 1229
Fax: 020 8977 9882
www.embroiderersguild.com

Tracy A Franklin
3 Fowlers Yard
Back Silver Street
Durham City DH1 3RA
Tel: 07946 401368
www.tracyafranklin.com
Email: tracy@tracyafranklin.com

Royal School of Needlework
Apartment 12A
Hampton Court Palace
East Molesey
Surrey KT8 9AU
Tel: 020 8943 1432
Fax: 020 8943 4910
www.royal-needlework.co.uk
Email: rnwork@intonet.co.uk

Museums and galleries

Allhallows Museum
High Street
Honiton
Devon EX14 1PG
Tel: 01404 44966
www.honitonmuseum.co.uk
Email: info@honitonmuseum

Blair Castle
Blair Atholl
Pitlochry
Perthshire PH18 5TL
Tel: 01796 481207
Fax: 01796 481487
www.blair-castle.co.uk
Email: office@blair-castle.co.uk

The Burrell Collection
2060 Pollokshaws Road
Glasgow G43 1AT
Tel: 0141 287 2550
Fax: 0141 287 2597
www.glasgowmuseums.com

Castle Howard
York
North Yorkshire YO60 6PT
Tel: 01653 648333
Fax: 01653 648529
www.castlehoward.co.uk
Email: house@castlehoward.co.uk

The Gallery of Costume
Platt Hall
Rusholme
Manchester M14 5LL
Tel: 0161 224 5217
Fax: 0161 256 3278
www.manchestergalleries.org.uk
Opening times by appointment
only

Glasgow Museums
Culture and Leisure Services
Martyrs School
Parson Street
Townhead
Glasgow G4 0PX
www.glasgowmuseums.com

Museum of Costume
Assembly Rooms
Bennett Street
Bath BA1 2QH
Tel: 01225 477789
www.museumofcostume.co.uk
Email:
costume_enquiries@bathnes.gov.uk

National Museums of Scotland
Chambers Street
Edinburgh EH1 1JF
Tel: 0131 247 4391
www.nms.ac.uk

Nottingham Castle Museum and Gallery
The Castle
Lenton Road
Nottingham NG1 6EL
Tel: 0115 9153700
Fax: 0115 9153653
Email: castle@ncmg.demon.co.uk

The Stewartry Museum
David Devereux
Museums Curator (Stewartry)
St. Mary Street
Kirkcudbright DG6 4AQ

Dumfries Museum
The Observatory
Rotchell Road
Dumfries DG2 7SW
Tel: 01387 253 374
Fax: 01387 265 081
www.dumgal.gov.uk/museums
Email:
dumfriesmuseum@dumgal.gov.uk

Traquair House
Innerleithen
Peeblesshire EH44 6PW
Tel: 01896 830323
Fax: 01896 830639
www.traquair.co.uk
Email: enquiries@traquair.co.uk

Ulster Folk & Transport Museum
Cultra
Holywood
County Down BT18 0EU
Tel: 02890 428428
Fax: 02890 428728
www.uftm.org.uk
Email:
uftmmarketing@btinternet.com

Victoria and Albert Museum
Cromwell Road
London SW7 2RL
Tel: 020 7942 2000
www.vam.ac.uk

The Whitworth Art Gallery
The University of Manchester
Oxford Road
Manchester M15 6ER
Tel: 0161 2757450
Fax: 0161 2757451
www.manchester.ac.uk/whitworth
Email:
whitworth@manchester.ac.uk

Witney Antiques
96–100 Corn Street
Witney
Oxfordshire
OX28 6BU
Tel: 01993 703902
Fax: 01993 779852
www.witneyantiques.com

Index

Deco Daisies

Small panel incorporating shadow quilting, net embroidery and surface work.
With the kind permission of the Royal School of Needlework.